Jesus of Nazareth—Christ of Faith

DATE DUE

Jesus of Nazareth—Christ of Faith

Peter Stuhlmacher

Translated by Siegfried S. Schatzmann

HENDRICKSON
PUBLISHERS
PEABODY, MASSACHUSETTS 01961-3473

Jesus von Nazareth—Christus des Glaubens
© 1988 by Calwer Verlag Stuttgart

English translation copyright © 1993 by
Hendrickson Publishers, Inc.
P. O. Box 3473
Peabody, Massachusetts 01961–3473
All rights reserved
Printed in the United States of America

ISBN 1–56563–009–2

Library of Congress Cataloging-in-Publication Data

Stuhlmacher, Peter
    [Jesus von Nazareth—Christus des Glaubens. English]
    Jesus of Nazareth—Christ of faith / Peter Stuhlmacher.
        p. cm.
    Includes bibliographical references and index.
    ISBN 1–56563–009–2 (pbk.)
    1. Jesus Christ—Person and offices. 2. Lord's Supper—Biblical
teaching. 3. Bible. N.T.—Criticism, interpretation, etc.
BT202.S8513 1993
292—dc20   93-5288
                                                                CIP

To Theo Sorg

ON APRIL 18, 1988

TABLE OF CONTENTS

Abbreviations

Ancient Works

Old Testament

Gen	Genesis
Exod	Exodus
Lev	Leviticus
Num	Numbers
Deut	Deuteronomy
Josh	Joshua
Judg	Judges
Ruth	Ruth
1-2 Sam	1-2 Samuel
1-2 Kgs	1-2 Kings
1-2 Chron	1-2 Chronicles
Ezra	Ezra
Neh	Nehemiah
Esth	Esther
Job	Job
Ps/Pss	Psalms
Prov	Proverbs

Eccl	Ecclesiastes
Song Sol	Song of Solomon
Isa	Isaiah
Jer	Jeremiah
Lam	Lamentations
Ezek	Ezekiel
Dan	Daniel
Hos	Hosea
Joel	Joel
Amos	Amos
Obad	Obadiah
Jonah	Jonah
Mic	Micah
Nah	Nahum
Hab	Habakkuk
Zeph	Zephaniah
Hag	Haggai
Zech	Zechariah
Mal	Malachi

New Testament

Matt	Matthew
Mark	Mark
Luke	Luke
John	John
Acts	Acts
Rom	Romans
1-2 Cor	1-2 Corinthians
Gal	Galatians
Eph	Ephesians
Phil	Philippians
Col	Colossians
1-2 Thess	1-2 Thessalonians
1-2 Tim	1-2 Timothy
Titus	Titus
Phlm	Philemon
Heb	Hebrews
Jas	James

1-2 Pet   1-2 Peter
1-2-3 John   1-2-3 John
Jude   Jude
Rev   Revelation

Apocrypha
    Sir   Sirach
    Wis   Wisdom of Solomon
    4 Ezra   4 Ezra

Apostolic Fathers
    Did.   Didache
    Ign. *Eph.*   Ignatius, *Letter to the Ephesians*
    Ign. *Smyrn.* Ignatius, *Letter to the Smyrneans*

Pseudepigrapha
    1 Enoch   Ethiopic Enoch
    Jub.   Jubilees
    Sib. Or.   Sibylline Oracles
    Pss. Sol.   Psalms of Solomon

Dead Sea Scrolls and Related Texts
    1QIsa^a first copy of Isaiah from Cave 1
    4QFlor   Florilegium from Cave 4
    4QpsDan ar^a first copy, Aramaic, of pseudo-Daniel from
                   Cave 4
    11QMelch   Melchizedek text from Cave 11

Tractates of Mishnah (m.) and Tosephta (t.)
    Ḥag.   Ḥagigah
    Ker.   Kerithoth
    Mak.   Makkoth
    Pesaḥ.   Pesaḥim
    Sanh.   Sanhedrin

Targum Material
    Tg. Isa.   Targum Isaiah
    Tg. Yer. I   Targum Yerušalmi I

Josephus

Ag. Ap.	Against Apion
Ant.	Jewish Antiquities
J.W.	The Jewish War

Periodicals, Series

ANRW	*Aufstieg und Niedergang der römischen Welt*
ConBNT	Coniectanea biblica, New Testament
EDNT	*Exegetical Dictionary of the New Testament,* ed. H. Balz and G. Schneider
EKKNT	Evangelisch-katholischer Kommentar zum Neuen Testament
EKL	*Evangelisches Kirchenlexikon*
EvT	*Evangelische Theologie*
GKC	Gesenius' Hebrew Grammar, ed. E. Kautzsch, trans. A. E. Cowley
JBT	*Jahrbuch für Biblische Theologie*
MeyerK	H. A. W. Meyer, ed., Kritisch-exegetischer Kommentar
NovTSup	Novum Testamentum, Supplements
NTD	Das Neue Testament Deutsch
NTS	*New Testament Studies*
QD	Quaestiones disputae
SBS	Stuttgarter Bibelstudien
SBT	Studies in Biblical Theology
Str-B	H. L. Strack and P. Billerbeck, *Kommentar zum Neuen Testament aus Talmud und Midrasch*
TBü	Theologische Bücherei
TDNT	*Theological Dictionary of the New Testament,* ed. G. Kittel and G. Friedrich, trans. and ed. G. W. Bromiley
THKNT	Theologischer Handkommentar zum Neuen Testament
TLZ	*Theologische Literaturzeitung*
TRu	*Theologische Rundschau*
TU	Texte und Untersuchungen

TZ	*Theologische Zeitschrift*
WUNT	Wissenschaftliche Untersuchungen zum Neuen Testament
ZTK	*Zeitschrift für Theologie und Kirche*

Other Abbreviations

ch.	chapter
esp.	especially
ET	English translation
MT	Masoretic text
Mt.	Mount
NRSV	New Revised Standard Version
n.s.	new series
NT	New Testament
OT	Old Testament
par.	and parallel(s)
RSV	Revised Standard Version
v(v).	verse(s)

Foreword for the English Edition

Five years after this volume's publication in Germany, Hendrickson Publishers, Inc., is making it accessible to English-speaking readers as well. The publishers deserve my expression of gratitude and Siegfried Schatzmann my appreciation for his excellent translation.

The backdrop to my presentation is the fundamental theological question of God's salvific acts in history which precede the Christian faith. The Gospels witness to the fact that God accomplished the eschatological salvation for Jews and Gentiles in and through Jesus Christ, prior to the existence of faith in Jesus Christ and of a Christian community. If one inquires into this witness and examines the historical knowledge that the Gospels have given to us concerning Jesus, their message is confirmed: Jesus of Nazareth appeared with the claim to be the messianic Son of man who was sent by God. In Jerusalem he endured the sacrificial death, so as to make atonement once for all, for Israel as well as the Gentiles who are guilty before God. By means of the resurrection on the third day God confirmed Jesus' sacrifice and made him to be the "Lord and Christ" of the whole world (cf. Acts 2:36). The early Christians' declaration that Jesus of Nazareth was the Christ was not a subsequent one; rather, as a result of Easter they learned to confess him as the messianic Son of God. He was the one who came from God, who ministered and suffered and who, according to Psalm 110:1, was exalted by God. Christology is effective in its declaration and is spiritually relevant to the extent that it accepts this biblical witness; if it does not follow this witness and instead adheres to some other modern portrait of Jesus, Christology loses its legitimacy.

Beyond my contribution which follows, those interested in the Lord's Supper ought to give their attention to the essay of my friend, Otfried Hofius, on "The Lord's Supper and the Lord's Supper Tradition. Reflections on 1 Corinthians 11:23b–25," in B. F. Meyer (ed.), *One Loaf—One Cup. Ecumenical Studies of 1 Corinthians 11 and Other Eucharistic Texts*, New Gospel Studies 6, Macon, Ga., 1993, pp. 75–115. His view of 1 Cor. 11:21, 33 and of the Lord's Supper tradition, passed on unaltered from Jesus via the early church to Corinth, makes such good sense that I incorporated it into the presentation of the history of the Lord's Supper in the first volume of my *Biblische Theologie des Neuen Testaments* (Göttingen: Vandenhoeck & Ruprecht, 1992). This volume also contains a comprehensive presentation of the proclamation of Jesus and its significance for the faith of the early Christians.

Tübingen, August 1993
Peter Stuhlmacher

1

JESUS OF NAZARETH AS CHRIST OF FAITH

FORMULATING THE QUESTION

TO CONFRONT TODAY THE QUESTIONS OF WHO WAS JESUS OF Nazareth and in what Christ do Christians believe means to wrestle with a framework of issues that has built up in the course of over one hundred years of theological and ecclesiastical discussion. Although the pressing importance of both questions continues,[1] they are not new but have concerned

---

[1] This importance is indicated in the never-ending sequence of new publications on the topic. As far as the English discussion is concerned, I refer to E. P. Sanders, *Jesus and Judaism* (Philadelphia: Fortress, 1985); James D. G. Dunn, *The Evidence for Jesus* (Philadelphia: Westminster, 1985); and James H. Charlesworth, "Research on the Historical Jesus Today: Jesus and the Pseudepigrapha, the Dead Sea Scrolls, the Nag Hammadi Codices, Josephus, and Archaeology," *Princeton Seminary Bulletin*, n.s. 6 (1985) 98–115. One can perceive the volatility of the German discussion in Hans-Friedrich Weiss, *Kerygma und Geschichte: Erwägungen zur Frage nach Jesus im Rahmen der Theologie des Neuen Testaments* (Berlin: Evangelische Verlagsanstalt, 1983); Gerd Theissen, *The Shadow of the Galilean: The Quest of the Historical Jesus in Narrative Form* (trans. John Bowden; Philadelphia: Fortress, 1987); Otto Betz, *Jesus: Der Messias Israels: Aufsätze zur biblischen Theologie* (WUNT 42; Tü-

Christians and non-Christians for a long time. In 1892 the dogmatic theologian Martin Kähler (1835–1912), who at that time taught in Halle, gave a lecture under a title that seemed curious at first: "The So-Called Historical Jesus and the Historic, Biblical Christ." In this position paper Kähler protested against the attempt of critical scholars who, by means of scholarly methods, "torturously extrapolated" from the four Gospels[2] an alleged historically reliable portrait of Jesus and then established it as the rule of faith in Jesus Christ. For Kähler the Christ of faith, the premise of the church from its inception as well as now, is the biblical Christ whose story the evangelists tell and to whom the other NT writers witness. The Gospels' portrait of Jesus is based on the impression that Jesus' disciples acquired during the years of their earthly ministry with him. This portrait does not contradict faith in Jesus Christ but strengthens it, and in its proclamation of faith the church may be content with this situation. If not, it needs to be.

Adolf Schlatter (1852–1938), who since 1898 served as professor of Dogmatics and New Testament in Tübingen, concurred with Kähler on this matter, but at the same time he redefined it decisively. Schlatter argued that the Christ of faith is none other than the historical Jesus, and pointed to Jesus' messianic sonship of God as the essential test case for this identity.[3] According to Schlatter Jesus of Nazareth appeared precisely as the Gospels record—with the claim to be the Son of God and Israel's Messiah; hence the apostles also confessed him as Son of God and Messiah. For Schlatter, the fundamental difference between the historical Jesus and the Christ of faith

---

bingen: J. C. B. Mohr [Paul Siebeck], 1987); and Eduard Schweizer, *Jesus Christ: The Man from Nazareth and the Exalted Lord* (Macon, Ga.: Mercer University Press, 1987); idem, "Jesus als Gleichnis Gottes," *Dialog aus der Mitte christlicher Theologie* (ed. Andreas Bsteh; Beiträge zur Religionstheologie 5; Mödling: St. Gabriel, 1987) 85–103.

[2] Martin Kähler, *Der sogenannte historische Jesus und der geschichtliche, biblische Christus* (ed. Ernst Wolf; TBü 2; Munich: C. Kaiser, 1956) 49; ET *The So-Called Historical Jesus and the Historic, Biblical Christ* (trans. Carl E. Braaten; Philadelphia: Fortress, 1969) 73.

[3] Adolf Schlatter, "Der Zweifel an der Messianität Jesu" (1907); now in A. Schlatter, *Zur Theologie des Neuen Testaments and zur Dogmatik* (ed. Ulrich Luck; TBü 41; Munich: C. Kaiser, 1969) 151–202.

arises only when one is not able and willing to conceptualize that the human Jesus already appeared as Messiah.

A few scholars, like Julius Schniewind,[4] Joachim Jeremias,[5] and Leonhard Goppelt,[6] followed (Kähler and) Schlatter; yet the majority of NT exegetes at home and abroad did not do so. They brushed aside Schlatter's warning and promptly fell into the aporias forecast by him. For them the unity of the portrait of Jesus broke apart,[7] so that they distinguished sharply between the historical Jesus on the one hand and the Christ who was not proclaimed and believed in until after Easter on the other. For instance, Rudolf Bultmann views the proclamation of the Jewish rabbi and prophet Jesus as part only of the presuppositions of a theology of the NT, rather than an essential ingredient of the development of the NT tradition of faith.[8]

The programmatic reflection upon the person and work of the human Jesus, initiated in the 1950s by Ernst Käsemann,[9] Günther Bornkamm,[10] and Ernst Fuchs,[11] has not yet yielded a

---

[4] Cf., e.g., his commentary, *Das Evangelium nach Markus* (10th ed.; NTD; Göttingen: Vandenhoeck & Ruprecht, 1963).

[5] *New Testament Theology: The Proclamation of Jesus* (trans. John Bowden; New York: Scribner's, 1971) 250–311.

[6] *Theology of the New Testament, Vol. 1: The Ministry of Jesus in Its Theological Significance* (trans. John Alsup; Grand Rapids: Eerdmans, 1981) 207–50.

[7] Schlatter writes ("Zweifel," 154): "If we take the messianic notion away from Jesus and we let only his companions and messengers proclaim him as the Christ, there emerges . . . a gap, the bridging of which will hardly be possible for the historical guild."

[8] Rudolf Bultmann, *Theology of the New Testament* (trans. Kendrick Grobel; 2 vols.; New York: Scribner's, 1951–55) 1:3: "*The message of Jesus* is a presupposition for the theology of the New Testament rather than a part of that theology itself. For New Testament theology consists in the unfolding of those ideas by means of which Christian faith makes sure of its own object, basis, and consequences. But Christian faith did not exist until there was a Christian kerygma; i.e., a kerygma proclaiming Jesus Christ—specifically Jesus Christ the Crucified and Risen One—to be God's eschatological act of salvation."

[9] Cf. Ernst Käsemann, "The Problem of the Historical Jesus," *Essays on New Testament Themes* (trans. W. J. Montague; SBT 1/41; Naperville, Ill.: Allenson, 1964) 15–47.

[10] Günther Bornkamm, *Jesus of Nazareth* (trans. Irene and Fraser McLuskey with James M. Robinson; London: Hodder and Stoughton, 1960).

[11] Ernst Fuchs, *Zur Frage nach dem historischen Jesus* (Tübingen: J. C. B. Mohr [Paul Siebeck], 1960) vol. 2; partial translation in *Studies of the Historical Jesus* (trans. Andrew Scobie; SBT 1/42; London: SCM, 1964).

tenable solution. Instead, a gaping chasm remains between the eschatological prophet Jesus, as seen in an allegedly historical portrait, and the Son of God, Jesus Christ, who was not confessed as the Christ of faith until after Easter. Many scholars link the two together by speaking of the indirect, pre-Easter, messianic claim to sovereignty on the part of Jesus and the direct confession of Jesus as Messiah and Christ in the post-Easter proclamation of the apostles.[12] As far as the biblical sources are concerned, this formula represents a relatively tolerable compromise, although it is not able to provide a permanent solution for the problem that Kähler and Schlatter pointed out. The question whether the young Christian community did not stylize Jesus as the saving Christ until later has indeed crucial soteriological significance. In the interest of truth and of faith, one has to clarify as meticulously as possible whether this was the case.[13]

---

[12] Käsemann writes, of Jesus: "Certainly he was a Jew and made the assumptions of Jewish piety, but at the same time he shatters this framework with his claim. The only category which does justice to his claim (quite independently of whether he used it himself and required it of others) is that in which his disciples themselves placed him—namely, that of the Messiah," "Problem," 38. Eduard Schweizer formulates it even more openly in *Jesus* (trans. David E. Green; Richmond, Va.: John Knox, 1971) 22: "The way God uses Jesus represents the culmination of all the Old Testament hopes concerning the Messiah, the Son of God, and the Servant of God. But Jesus keeps all the possibilities open; he refuses to use titles which of necessity define and delimit, to make God's free action an object of human thought, placing it at the disposal of the human mind. By his very act of avoiding all common labels, Jesus keeps free the heart of the person who encounters him. He wants to enter into this heart himself, in all the reality of what he says and does, not as an image already formed before he himself has a chance to encounter the person." In his most recent publications on the topic, *Jesus Christ*, "Jesus als Gleichnis Gottes," Schweizer varies slightly from this viewpoint and suggests that we understand "Jesus as the parable of God"; as far as the issue itself is concerned, this is an excellent suggestion.

[13] Schlatter formulates aptly and at the same time pointedly, *Das christliche Dogma* (3rd ed.; Stuttgart: Calwer, 1977) 122: "A Christology in which we attribute deity to Jesus via our faith, or a doctrine of justification in which we declare ourselves justified by means of the creative power of our faith, are superstitions." In this context, see my essay, "Adolf Schlatter als Bibelausleger," *Versöhnung, Gesetz und Gerechtigkeit* (Göttingen: Vandenhoeck & Ruprecht, 1981) 285ff. (partial ET in "Adolf Schlatter's Interpretation of Scripture," *NTS* 24 [4, 1978] 441–43).

The more the Christian-Jewish dialogue (which fortunately has been initiated again) pleads for a diminished portrait of Jesus as common guide, the less helpful the solution in vogue becomes. The Jewish part is discovering (and rightly so) a Jesus in the Gospels who lived, worked, and suffered as a Jew and is indeed ready to see this Jesus as "one of the prophets" (Mark 8:28), if not even "more than" a prophet and a teacher of wisdom who is "more than Solomon" (Matt 12:41–42).[14] Whether the human Jesus was (and remains) Israel's Messiah is of course left open or rejected.[15] Indeed, the Jewish partners in the dialogue do not need to accept this doctrine at all because the Christian partners cooperate with them by means of their critical portrait of Jesus, by dating the confession of Jesus as Messiah and Son of God beginning with Easter, and by not allowing the human Jesus himself to make a direct messianic claim.[16] In view of this dialogue the old view of Schlatter appears to be either antiquated or—even worse—tainted as anti-Semitic and hence evil.

Nonetheless, Schlatter's view is correct. Here I concur with the historical assessment of my friends and colleagues in Tü-

---

[14] Cf. David Flusser, *Jesus* (trans. Ronald Walls; New York: Herder and Herder, 1969); Schalom Ben-Chorin, *Bruder Jesus: Der Nazarener in jüdischer Sicht* (Munich: 1967); Pinchas Lapide and Ulrich Luz, *Jesus in Two Perspectives: A Jewish-Christian Dialog* (trans. Lawrence W. Denef; Minneapolis: Augsburg, 1985).

[15] Flusser, *Jesus*, 99ff., argues that in the final analysis Jesus identified himself with the messianically understood Jewish Son of man; Ben-Chorin, *Bruder Jesus*, p. 108, admits (with Rudolf Bultmann) "that Jesus did not claim to be the Messiah"; Lapide, *Jesus*, 55–56, cites Jürgen Moltmann with approval: "Through his crucifixion Jesus has become the Saviour of the Gentiles. But in his Parousia he will also manifest himself as Israel's Messiah." He formulates it even more pointedly in his essay, "Der Messias Israels?" *Umkehr und Erneuerung* (ed. Bertold Klappert and Helmut Starck; 1980) 242: "Jesus was *not* Israel's Messiah and yet became the savior of the Gentiles."

[16] This is verified classically in the citations from critical NT scholars like Rudolf Bultmann, Eduard Schweizer, Hans Conzelmann, Ernst Käsemann, Günther Bornkamm, Günther Klein, and Eduard Lohse, as well as in the works of Pinchas Lapide. See, e.g., Lapide, *Jesus*, 29–30, 33–34, 43; idem, *Wer war schuld an Jesu Tod?* (Gütersloh: Mohn, 1987) 59, 61–62, 66, 77, etc. For the same procedure in the English discussion, see Donald A. Hagner, *The Jewish Reclamation of Jesus* (Grand Rapids: Zondervan, 1984) 242–71.

bingen, Otto Betz[17] and Martin Hengel.[18] Even if today one views the Gospels, as well as the remaining NT books, with considerably greater differentiation than Schlatter thought necessary,[19] he deserves agreement in the main issue. Without seeing and acknowledging that the human Jesus already laid claim to

---

[17] Cf. Otto Betz, "Die Frage nach dem messianischen Bewusstsein Jesu," *Jesus*, 140–68; idem, *What Do We Know about Jesus?* (trans. Margaret Kohl; London: SCM, 1968) 83 ff.

[18] Martin Hengel, *The Charismatic Leader and His Followers* (trans. James Greig; New York: Crossroad, 1981) 42–50, 80–83; idem, *The Son of God: The Origin of Christology and the History of Jewish-Hellenistic Religion* (trans. John Bowden; Philadelphia: Fortress, 1976) 89ff.; idem, "Jesus als messianischer Lehrer der Weisheit und die Anfänge der Christologie," *Sagesse et Religion*, Colloque de Strasbourg (Paris: Presses universitaires de France, 1979) 175, 180ff.; idem, "Zur Matthäischen Bergpredigt und ihrem jüdischen Hintergrund," *TRu* 52 (1987) 377; idem, *The Atonement* (trans. John Bowden; Philadelphia: Fortress, 1981) 71–73. Likewise both I. Howard Marshall, *The Origins of New Testament Christology* (Downers Grove, Ill.: InterVarsity, 1976) 63–96; and Petr Pokorný, *The Genesis of Christology* (trans. Markus Lefébure; Edinburgh: T. & T. Clark, 1987) 38–59; begin carefully with the assertion that the historical origin of the NT Christology has to be located already in Jesus' own messianic claim.

[19] In his *Rückblick auf meine Lebensarbeit* (2d ed.; 1977) 233–34, Schlatter writes: "My attempt to provide my theology with a form that is clear to the church had its premise in the fact that I saw the history of Jesus as a totality. I did not have a Johannine Christ alongside a synoptic one, nor a prophet who gave the Sermon on the Mount alongside a Christ who bore the cross, nor did I dissect his consciousness into various 'circles' that traversed his consciousness alternately and resulted in several Gospels. I perceived him to have *one* goal and *one* mission, generating the entire wealth of his word and deed. I did not see this unity as an artistic work of my own harmonization, obscuring the specificity of the particular words and events, but as the result of an historical understanding that was as concrete as possible. It seemed to me that I was justified in the attempt to show it to others in the same manner. Neither did I see a cleft between Jesus' ministry and that of his messengers, between Israel's call to repentance and the founding of the Christian church, between Peter's ministry in Jerusalem and Paul's among the Greeks. Rather I had in my possession a unified New Testament, again not because it did not have unity until I applied my artistry and apologetic, but because an integral history, produced at every point by the same powers, brought forth the community and its documents, gathered by the disciples after Jesus' departure. For this reason I posited my description of the New Testament community alongside those of others that are mutilated by innumerable contradictions." As correct as Schlatter's basic ideas are, here he does underestimate the difficult conflicts that occurred in early Christianity about the correct understanding of Jesus and the way of faith. For this reason one must distinguish more clearly than he did between historical and biblical-dogmatic text assessments.

being the messianic Son of man whom God sent to Israel, one cannot make sense historically of Jesus' ministry, or of even the passion narrative. The apostles did not attribute characteristics and behavior patterns to Jesus subsequent to Easter that were not his in his humanity (nor that he claimed to possess); the Christian community's post-Easter confession of Jesus as Son of God and Messiah confirms and acknowledges who Jesus claimed to be historically and who he was and remains for faith. God's history in and with Jesus, the Christ of God, is pre-positioned (*vorgegeben*) to the Christian faith. It maintains and determines this faith and is not merely called into existence by it.[20]

FORMULATING THE PROBLEM AND THE TASK

In the light of what has been argued thus far, many may ask whether this whole debate represents more than merely a typical feud among professors, with no significance for church practice. It is indeed possible to take this view, but one should not pass this debate off too lightly, for the question of what right Christians have to confess Jesus as Christ and Son of God concerns all Christians (and all non-Christians as well, to the extent that they claim the privilege to reject or consider un-important the Christians' confession).

One can easily recognize that these are genuine questions of faith when one attempts to link two post-Easter confessions of Jesus as Christ and Son of God found in the NT with the Jesus tradition of the Gospels, and furthermore when one considers that the Gospels themselves do not report uniformly about Jesus and his passion. Both instances clearly take considerable mental effort to arrive at a biblical portrait of Jesus that is convincing on its own merits.

---

[20] Cf. Käsemann, "Problem," 34: "The Easter faith was the foundation of the Christian kerygma but was not the first or only source of its content. Rather, it was the Easter faith which took cognizance of the fact that God acted before we became believers and which testified to this fact by encapsulating the earthly history of Jesus in its proclamation." Bornkamm, *Jesus*, 11–23, and Weiss, *Kerygma*, 102–5, argue similarly. In my view gospel research needs to work out Käsemann's perspective consistently.

Two Post-Easter Confessions of Christ

In its three articles the so-called Apostles' Creed, prevalent in contemporary churches, claims to be a summation of the essential testimonial statements of the Holy Scriptures for the Christian faith. The second article of the creed has its decisive models in the early Christian dogmas and confessions of Jesus as Son of God and Messiah already formulated in the Bible. Here I focus on two of these confessions. Paul cites the first one in 1 Corinthians 15, and he himself declares it to be characteristic for all apostles; the second one occurs in 1 Timothy and is characteristic for the church of the postapostolic era.

In 1 Corinthians 15:3–8 Paul writes to the community in Corinth:

> For I handed on to you as of first importance [as doctrine] what I in turn had received [as doctrine]: that Christ died for our sins in accordance with the scriptures, and that he was buried, and that he was raised on the third day in accordance with the scriptures, and that he appeared to Cephas [Peter], then to the twelve. Then he appeared to more than five hundred brothers and sisters at one time, most of whom are still alive [note: Paul wrote 1 Corinthians from Ephesus ca. AD 54/55], though some have died. Then he appeared to James, then to all the apostles. Last of all, as to one untimely born, he appeared also to me (NRSV).

Verses 3–5 are a terse didactic formulation of the "gospel" (cf. v. 1) that originated in the earliest years following Jesus' death and resurrection. According to Paul, all the apostles enumerated by him proclaim this gospel (cf. v. 11). Central to this gospel is the death of *Christ* for our sins, his burial, his resurrection by God on the third day, and his appearances to Peter, the Twelve, and other apostles. The death and resurrection of Jesus transpired, as the text points out emphatically, "in accordance with the scriptures," that is, in keeping with the will of God as delineated and authenticated in the OT. According to vv. 3–5 Jesus' death for our sins and his resurrection by God constitute the center of the gospel of Christ.

The confessional text of 1 Timothy 2:5–6 is similar and yet somewhat different in perspective:

For there is one God; there is also one mediator between God and humankind, Christ Jesus, himself human, who gave himself a ransom for all—this was attested at the right time (NRSV).

According to this text Jesus is the one God-appointed mediator between God and humans, who sealed his divine mission by means of delivering up his life for all and who established the witness of the gospel at the moment in time that God appointed (cf. v. 6 with 2 Tim 1:8 and Gal 4:4). This is the gospel that Paul and the leaders of the community(-ies) are to proclaim.

The two formulaic texts of 1 Corinthians 15 and 1 Timothy 2 take a retrospective glance at Jesus from Easter, and in his passion they see the decisive climax of his mission as Messiah and Son of man, a climax leading the believers to salvation. The pondering of the passion tradition arises naturally in the perspective of both texts, and one can contest it only artificially (which still happens occasionally, however).[21]

Precisely this sharp focus upon the passion presents even interested Christians today with considerable dilemmas. From the perspective of contemporary ways of thinking, the narrative of the divinely willed, sacrificial death of Jesus appears to be not only hard to grasp but also offensive. Why was the sacrifice of the Son of God on the cross required in order to procure forgiveness of our sins? A God who allows his own son to be executed on the cross and to forgive sinners only as a consequence of it seems cruel and alien, like Molech (cf. Lev 18:21; Isa 30:33)—not a God of love. Whether one can overcome this offense is one of the most significant questions of comprehension today. For those who are not able to understand Jesus' passion the early Christian confession of Jesus as the Christ of

---

[21] This happens, for instance, by doubting whether Paul had any knowledge of the (synoptic) tradition of the passion at all. If one takes this view, one may also contest that 1 Cor 15:3–5 indeed focuses on the tradition of the Lord's Supper and of the burial. For instance, Joachim Gnilka argues that the tradition of Mark 16:1–8 arose by "reaching back to the structure of faith in 1 Cor 15:3–5 and describing the message of the resurrection by means of the empty tomb," and a little later, in the sense of an "insurmountable argument"(!) he refers to "the absence of a reference to the empty tomb in the ancient confessional formula of 1 Cor 15:3–5," *Das Evangelium nach Markus* (EKKNT; Neukirchen-Vluyn: Neukirchener, 1979) 2.339, 346).

God (and hence the Christian confession as a whole) must remain alien. Thus one faces a genuine problem of faith.

The Diverse Witness of the Gospels and the Need for Critical Evaluation

All four Gospels agree with the early Christian confessions of Jesus as the Christ of God and as the mediator between God and humans in that they all accord great importance to the narrative of Jesus' passion. Martin Kähler coined the striking formulation: "To state the matter somewhat provocatively, one could call the Gospels passion narratives with extended introductions." [22] Apart from understanding the passion story one can have no understanding of the Gospels. Yet the Gospels do not recount uniformly the passion of Jesus. The major differences are between the Gospel of John and the first three Gospels (although the [pre-]Lukan passion narrative is already distinct from that of Mark and Matthew and is related to the Johannine passion). Differences in dating and emphasis are conspicuous to interpreters and have given them trouble ever since the days of the early church. According to the Gospel of John, Jesus dies on the cross at precisely the hour when the Passover lambs are killed in the temple in order to prepare them for the Passover meal in the evening. On that evening, Mark, Matthew, and Luke recount that Jesus celebrates the Passover meal with his twelve disciples, but John depicts Jesus as already dead. In the Fourth Gospel, therefore, one looks in vain for a Lord's Supper account like the one offered in the first three Gospels and Paul (in 1 Cor 11:23ff.). At the same time, except for a few allusions (cf. John 13:21; 19:28), John corrects all the expressions of human weakness that are familiar from the passion narratives of the other Gospels. Thus Jesus' trembling with fear in Gethsemane (cf. Mark 14:32–42 par.) is turned virtually into its opposite in John 12:27–33 and 18:2–11. The gripping scene of Jesus' collapse under the cross that he is dragging to Golgotha, the soldiers forcing Simon of Cyrene to carry the cross for Jesus (cf. Mark

---

[22] Kähler, *So-Called Historical Jesus*, 80 n. 11.

15:20–21), is replaced in John 19:17 with the pointed remark that Jesus "carried his own cross," that is, by his own effort. Instead of the cry of dereliction from Psalm 22:2, "My God, my God, why have you forsaken me?" (Mark 15:34 and Matt 27:46), according to John the last words of Jesus on the cross are: "It is finished" (John 19:30). In view of this serious shift in emphasis over against the first three Gospels, one has no alternative other than to read the presentation of the passion in the four Gospels critically and not simply to overplay the differences harmonistically.

But the first three Gospels also have differences that one must consider and explain. For instance, why does the Gospel of Mark begin only with the account of the appearance of John the Baptist and Jesus' baptism, while Matthew and Luke offer their famous antecedent stories (among them the Christmas story in Luke 2)? How does one explain the unified Sermon on the Mount in Matthew 5–7 and its parallels in Luke which are divided into the brief so-called Sermon on the Plain (Luke 6:17–49), and various sayings of Jesus scattered throughout the Gospel of Luke? Mark says nothing at all about a Sermon on the Mount or a Sermon on the Plain, nor does he pass on the Lord's Prayer, given in Matthew 6:9–13 and in Luke 12:2–4. Conversely, the notation that Jesus' family left Nazareth to seize Jesus because they were of the opinion that "he is out of his mind" (Mark 3:20–21) occurs only in Mark. One's intention to read the passion narrative critically, therefore, needs to be widened to include the Gospels in their totality if one truly wants to obtain a relatively reliable portrait of Jesus.

Incidentally, such critical reading does not do any injustice to the Bible. First, in his conclusion to 1 Thessalonians, Paul already appealed to the community not to despise prophetic witnesses but to test everything and to hold fast (only) what is good (1 Thess 5:20–21; similarly cf. Rom 12:2). Second, 1 Peter calls upon the Christians always to be prepared "to make a defense to any one who calls you to account for the hope that is in you" (1 Pet 3:15). But in the modern context and in the present discussion one can give an account only if one makes clear, as far as possible, how Jesus' proclamation and faith in him relate to one another and what one is to make of the biblical witness on the whole. In order to do justice to 1 Peter 3:15, critical historical work in the Holy Scriptures is indispensable in the current situation of dialogue, which is characterized by a veritable chaos of opinions, both inside and outside the church.

FROM THE PROCLAMATION OF JESUS TO FAITH IN JESUS CHRIST

To retrace the way from the proclamation of Jesus to faith in Jesus Christ, as expressed in exemplary form in the confessions of faith mentioned previously, means to venture a critical reconstruction taking into account those problems and differences among biblical sources to which I have drawn attention. Every reconstruction has to follow particular methodological guidelines that are as much subject to the discussion as the reconstructed issue itself. To enable the reader to follow me critically, I first address the principles of reconstruction that guide me, and only then embark upon the presentation of the issue under discussion.

The Principles of Reconstruction

In determining the relationship of the four Gospels to one another, I begin with the assumption (widely recognized, though not for that reason unquestionably valid) that the earliest Gospel is the one to which John Mark (see Acts 12:12; 13:5, 13; 15:37–39; Phlm 24; Col 4:10; 2 Tim 4:11; 1 Pet 5:13) applied the final editing, probably in Rome, prior to the destruction of Jerusalem by Roman troops in AD 70—the Gospel of Mark. It is based upon the tradition of Peter and of other early apostolic narratival and proclamational traditions.[23] The Gospels according to Matthew and Luke used this Gospel of Mark as source and model. But they incorporated into their Gospels additional

---

[23] On the pre-AD 70 origin of the Gospel of Mark and its traditions, see Martin Hengel, *Studies in the Gospel of Mark* (trans. John Bowden; Philadelphia: Fortress, 1985).

material from a "source of sayings and discourses" that served Christian teachers and prophetic missionaries in Palestine and Syria as a manual in their ministry of proclamation. For instance, from this source, generally identified simply as Q, for German *Quelle*, originates the essential founding of the tradition of the Sermon on the Mount (and the Lukan Sermon on the Plain). If one combines the tradition of the source of sayings and discourses with the presentation of Mark, one gains a relatively reliable portrait of the proclamation and work of Jesus. One can supplement this portrait further by the narratives from the traditions transmitted uniquely by Mark, Matthew, or Luke, the so-called special material of each Gospel. This portrait is reliable because the tradition of narrative and vocabulary, handed down in the sayings source and in Mark, and the traditions of the special material are based upon the recollection of Peter and of those women and men who accompanied Jesus during his earthly ministry, who after Easter were commissioned by the resurrected Christ to be his apostles, and who constituted the nucleus of the earliest community. The continuity of the circle of disciples from the pre-Easter to the post-Easter period safeguards the continuity of the Jesus tradition.[24]

Over against the first three Gospels, the Gospel of John represents a new phase of tradition. It assumes (especially) the Petrine tradition already mentioned as familiar, continues it critically, and supplements it in the perspective of faith. Based on the person and witness of the "disciple whom Jesus loved" (cf. John 13:23; 19:26; 20:2; 21:7, 20), the Fourth Gospel intends to present the mission and work of Jesus in the light of the insight, granted by the Holy Spirit only after Easter, into the truth of the revelation (cf. John 14:16–17, 26; 15:26; 16:7–14). For precisely this reason the early church considered the Gospel of John as the true, spiritual, main Gospel, whose witness of truth encompasses and culminates that of the other three Gospels.

---

[24] This continuity is stressed correctly by Birger Gerhardsson, *The Origins of the Gospel Traditions* (Philadelphia: Fortress, 1979); and by Rainer Riesner, *Jesus als Lehrer* (2d ed.; Tübingen: J. C. B. Mohr [Paul Siebeck], 1984); and summarized in idem, "Der Ursprung der Jesus-Überlieferung," *TZ* 38 (1982) 493–513.

Along with this historical orientation of the relationship among the four Gospels, another principle of reconstruction guiding me is the realization that a Christian NT never existed separate or detachable from the OT (except in the case of the "reformer" Marcion, who was excommunicated from the Roman community in AD 144), hence it can exist only in an artificial manner. This realization is confirmed on every level of the NT tradition of faith, as well as from the history of the Christian Bible. Jesus and his disciples, including Paul, who was called belatedly, were Jews by birth. They were raised in Israel's faith and read the Law, the Prophets, and the Psalms (Luke 24:44) as the Holy Scriptures, and—customary at that time—they had memorized it in part. Through Jesus and the apostles these OT "Holy Scriptures" also became the Bible of the communities believing in Jesus. Before a single NT document was written, the earliest Christian communities read the OT (in Hebrew and Greek) as Holy Scripture and interpreted it christologically. From the Christian perspective the NT supplements the OT and yields its decisive interpretive key, yet it cannot and will not supplant the OT.

Thus in the modern context one can reconstruct the way from Jesus' proclamation to faith in Jesus Christ only by beginning with a critical overall perspective of the NT sources and by viewing Jesus at the same time in the light of the OT witness of God's uniqueness, his promises for Israel, and his announcement of the messianic redeemer to come. To formulate it even more distinctly: The OT witness of revelation signals the decisive direction in which one should focus in order to understand historically and biblically the way from the proclamation of Jesus to faith in Jesus.[25] Those who ignore this perspective cannot adequately answer the question before us.

---

[25] Classically already in Kähler, *So-Called Historical Jesus*, 85: "Nevertheless, the fact remains that Christ can never be evaluated apart from the Old Testament. It is an error to think and say that the situation is one where Christ merely throws light upon the Old Testament. Just as Jesus could appear as the Messiah only among the Jews, so we, too, would be totally unable to appreciate him if we had not been reared on the Old Testament"; and a little later (86): "It still holds true that this Jesus is in fact the Messiah whose Spirit spoke through the prophets (1 Pet 1:11). The historic Christ cannot be portrayed apart from

Jesus' Message Concerning God, Repentance, and Faith

As the Lukan prehistory indicates and many other Gospel texts confirm, Jesus was well acquainted with the OT and the Jewish faith from the beginning (cf. Luke 2:41–51 and John 7:15–17). John the Baptist's (his cousin) preaching of repentance called Jesus, at the approximate age of thirty, to the Jordan and prompted him to be baptized. For Jesus the baptism in the Jordan was not merely a seal of turning to a new life, pleasing to God, in anticipation of the imminent eschatological judgment, as it was for the others baptized by John; rather it signified the act of detaching himself from all family ties and inaugurating his public, messianic ministry. Jesus' experience with the Spirit at his baptism caused him to recognize that the time had now come for public ministry. To minister in public means to call people, by one's own authority, to repentance and to faith in the message of the impending dawn of the kingdom of God. Jesus' public proclamation began: "The time is fulfilled, and the kingdom of God is at hand; repent and believe in the gospel" (Mark 1:15).

For Jesus and his Jewish contemporaries the identity of God and of God's kingdom arose from the OT and the Jewish life of faith. One need only recall the first commandment and its preamble: "I am the Lord your God, who brought you out of Egypt, out of the land of slavery. You shall have no other gods before me" (Exod 20:2–3). Every devout Jew prayed (and prays) daily the confessional prayer based on Deuteronomy 6:4–5 and other passages (e.g., Deut 11:13–21; Num 15:37–41): "Hear, O Israel: The Lord our God, the Lord is one. Therefore love the Lord your God with all your heart and with all your soul and with all your strength." The Psalms (e.g., in Ps 145) or Daniel (4:3, 34 [most translations; JB, MT 3:33; 4:31]) address the present rule of God. One hears about the impending inauguration of God's kingdom over all the world, for instance, in (the so-called Second) Isaiah (52:7) and in the Jewish

---

the Old Testament and without taking into account the Old Testament background as well as the Old Testament coloring of his life as he lived it in the presence of, and in, his Father."

prayer tradition. Just as the devout prayed (and are praying) the Shema ("Hear, O Israel!"), since the time of Jesus they have been praying daily the so-called Eighteen Benedictions. The eleventh benediction says: "Establish our judges again as formerly and our counselors as in the beginning, and be king over us, you alone. Blessed are you, Lord, who loves justice." Jesus announces the impending breaking in of the kingdom of the one God to whom the OT witnesses in such a way that his audience is to give their complete and undivided attention to the coming of this one God as judge and savior of his chosen people.

Although unusual from the Jewish perspective, Jesus characteristically addresses the one, coming God directly as "Father" (cf. Luke 10:21 par; Mark 14:36 par.), and in the Lord's Prayer he even allows his disciples to share in this relationship with God. Precisely by means of this new kind of address to God as *Father*, Jesus proves to be the Son of God. Jesus teaches them to recognize and heed anew what this one, coming God bestows upon those who are motivated to hear Jesus, and what he demands from them. In his (benevolent) dialogue with a scribe concerning the question of the most important commandment among the 613 directives that constitute the law, according to rabbinic count (248 commandments and 365 prohibitions), Jesus responds by essentially combining two commandments, which was by no means common in Palestine: "The most important [commandment] is: 'Hear, O Israel: The Lord our God, the Lord is one; and you shall love the Lord your God with all your heart, and with all your soul, and with all your mind, and with all your strength.' The second one is this, 'You shall love your neighbor as yourself.' There is no other commandment greater than these" (Mark 12:29–31). For Jesus the twofold commandment of loving God and neighbor determines the will of God in its entirety. If Jesus makes the commandment of love central, he does it on the basis that the one God, his Father, is a God of love and delights more in the repentance and life of the poor, the godforsaken, and the sinners than in their destruction.

The well-known story of Jesus' visit with the tax collector Zacchaeus in Jericho (Luke 19:1–10) illustrates clearly and concretely what the sinners' repentance, brought about by Jesus, looked like. Over the indignation of some citizens of the town, Jesus invites himself to stay with the tax collector (of all people), who was deemed as unjust and godless, and Zacchaeus receives him gladly. The encounter prompts Zacchaeus to give half of his possessions to the poor and to repay those he had defrauded by making fourfold amends. Jesus accepts this promise with satisfaction and salutes the man as a "son of Abraham" who has been reclaimed for fellowship with God. The entire incident illustrates that "the Son of man came to seek and to save the lost" (Luke 19:10).

Repentance in Jesus' understanding, then, means two things. First, arising from the encounter with Jesus, it means turning away from the old way of life in injustice and alienation from God, and turning toward the one God and Father, to whom Jesus himself belongs. Second, it means complying with the will of this God by acts of love and righteousness.

The Sermon on the Mount shows in great detail, and the famous parable of the Judgment of the Nations in Matthew 25:31–46 underscores, just how important acts of love and righteousness were and remain for Jesus.[26] To practice love and righteousness means to feed the hungry, to give drink to the thirsty, to provide shelter for the homeless, to clothe the naked, to care for the sick, and to visit those in prison—always and wherever it is necessary (cf. Isa 58:6–7). Here Jesus identifies with the suffering in such a way that he considers every good deed done to them as done to him.

Jesus' invitation and call to repentance, however, also has its quite natural underside; one must not squander it. Those who reject his call to repentance remain alienated from God and have to bear the consequences of their reserve themselves. Jesus teaches that these consequences will catch up with the unrepentant no later than on the day of judgment; see, for instance, his declaration of woe over the two Galilean towns Chorazin and Bethsaida that reject him (Matt 11:20–24 par. Luke 10:12–15).

---

[26]On the roots of this parable in Jesus, and on the Jewish traditions involved in it, see Johannes Friedrich, *Gott im Bruder?* (Stuttgart: Calwer, 1977).

Jesus' call of repentance comes on the horizon of the approaching day of judgment.

Through his proclamation and his own behavior Jesus makes clear how much the one God, whom Jesus serves and proclaims, desires to posit mercy and forgiveness of sins before judgment and punishment. The three parables grouped together in Luke 15—the Lost Sheep, the Lost Son, and the Lost Coin—document most beautifully Jesus' understanding that heaven (i.e., God) rejoices more over the repentance of a single sinner than over the repentance of ninety-nine who are righteous or who are already on the way of righteousness (Luke 15:7). In the occasions of table fellowship that he shares with them before God, Jesus shows just how welcome sinners and lost people are in God's fellowship (cf. Mark 2:15–16; Luke 15:2).

Jesus' miracles of healing are likewise part of this context. To the indignation of some scribes he not only heals the sick in the power (of the Spirit) of God that inspires him, but he even dares to forgive their sins. This is documented in the account of the healing of the paralytic in Capernaum in Mark 2:1–12:

> When he returned to Capernaum after some days, it was reported that he was at [Peter's] home [again]. So many gathered around that there was no longer room for them, not even in front of the door; and he was speaking the word to them. Then some people came, bringing to him a paralyzed man, carried by four of them. And when they could not bring him to Jesus because of the crowd, they removed the roof above him; and after having dug through it, they let down the mat on which the paralytic lay. When Jesus saw their faith, he said to the paralytic, "Son [of God], your sins are forgiven." Now some of the scribes were sitting there, questioning in their hearts, "Why does this fellow speak in this way? It is blasphemy [against God]! Who can forgive sins but God alone?" At once Jesus perceived in his spirit that they were discussing these questions among themselves; and he said to them, "Why do you raise such questions in your hearts? Which is easier, to say to the paralytic, 'Your sins are forgiven,' or to say, 'Stand up and take your mat and walk'? But so that you may know that the Son of Man has authority on earth to forgive sins"—he said to the paralytic—"I say to you, stand up, take your mat and go to your home." And he stood up,

and immediately took the mat and went out before all of them; so that they were all amazed and glorified God, saying, "We have never seen anything like this!" (NRSV).

Nothing in this story is incredible; the local particulars have been preserved in Capernaum to this day. One sees how Jesus, who calls himself "Son of man," responds to the confidence—the text speaks of "faith"—that the four who carried the paralytic had in him, namely, with the statement of forgiveness and with healing by the spoken word. This statement is particularly shocking because Jesus thereby transgresses the right to forgive sins that (in the view of the Jews) is God's prerogative alone. Against this horizon the narrative clearly signals the following: Through the word Jesus utters God takes hold of the one who is ill and heals him in body and soul. Jesus brings to life Psalm 103:2: "Praise the Lord, O my soul . . . who forgives all your sins and heals all your diseases."[27]

This incident in Capernaum is not a unique case, however; it represents Jesus' characteristic disposition. A second example from the Gospel of Mark is instructive in this regard: the healing of the epileptic and the subsequent discussion between Jesus and his disciples (Mark 9:14–29). While Jesus is absent a father brings his son who suffers from epileptic fits to Jesus' disciples, who endeavor in vain to help the child. When Jesus returns they inform him about the difficulty of this case. He steps up and asks the father:

> "How long has this been happening to him?" And he said, "From childhood. It [the evil demon of sickness] has often cast him into the fire and into the water, to destroy him; but if you are able to do anything, [then] have pity on us and help us." Jesus said to him, "If you are able! — All things can be done for the one who believes." Immediately the father of the child cried out, "I believe; help my unbelief!" When Jesus saw that a crowd came running together, he rebuked the unclean spirit, saying to it, "You spirit that keeps this boy from speaking and hearing, I command you, come out of him, and never enter him again!" After crying out and convulsing him [the child] terribly, it [the spirit] came out, and the boy

---

[27] Cf. Otto Betz, "Jesu Lieblingspsalm," *Jesus,* 198–99.

was like a corpse, so that most of them said, "He is dead." But Jesus took him by the hand and lifted him up, and he was able to stand. When he had entered the house, his disciples asked him privately, "Why could we not cast it out?" He said to them, "This kind [of spirit] can come out only through prayer" (NRSV).

The issue in this graphically narrated story is not Jesus' faith, as many interpreters argue; Jesus' special relationship with God is never designated by the term *faith* in the four Gospels.[28] Rather, one sees Jesus once again on God's side. He challenges the father to faith in God for whom, according to Jesus' own words, all things are possible (cf. Mark 14:36). When the father then confesses his faith and pleads for his unbelief to be remedied, Jesus, in the name of God, turns to the one who is ill and heals him by his word. Although epilepsy was considered incurable in antiquity, the activity of God who can truly do all things is carried out through Jesus' word and deed. In similar situations the disciples are able to petition this activity of God only through prayer; it is not a matter of their own power. In the context of this narrative, faith means to petition almighty God to act, through Jesus, on behalf of the one praying.

The Gospel of Matthew adds another saying from the sayings source (see above) to Jesus' concluding discussion with the disciples: "For truly, I say to you, if you have faith as a grain of mustard seed, you will say to this mountain, 'Move from here to there,' and it will move; and nothing will be impossible to you" (Matt 17:20). This saying about mountain-moving faith occurs in a different context in the Gospel of Mark. During his final stay in Jerusalem Jesus impresses upon his disciples who are marvelling about the cursing and withering of the fig tree: "Have faith in God. Truly, I say to you, whoever says to this mountain, 'Be taken up and cast into the sea,' and does not doubt in his heart, but believes that what he says will come to pass, it will be done for him. Therefore I tell you, whatever you ask in prayer, believe that you have received it, and it will be yours" (Mark 11:22–24).

---

[28] Only Heb 12:2 designates Jesus as "the author and finisher of faith," but in doing so follows the early Jewish model of faith, as ch. 11 shows.

According to the OT, only God, the creator and judge, has power to form mountains (cf. Ps 65:7) and to move them (Job 9:5; Jer 51:25), and his word of creation and judgment accomplishes what he commands (Pss 33:9; 148:5; Isa 55:11). Thus what Jesus has in mind is clear. If the disciples pray with undivided heart, almighty God assists them, so that spirits and worlds are literally separated on account of their work. The saying aims at the disciples' key function (cf. Matt 18:18), and in this sense Paul refers to it in 1 Corinthians 13:2 and argues that one needs to augment it (by love).

The Gospel of Luke offers a parallel saying in 17:6. Jesus says to his disciples, who ask him to grant them faith: "If you had faith [only as big] as a grain of mustard seed, you could say to this mulberry tree, 'Be rooted up, and be planted in the sea,' and it would obey you." Once again the meaning is very similar. The mulberry (sycamore-fig) is a tree with particularly deep roots. Uprooting trees is an OT word picture for the execution of judgment (cf. Jer 1:10 and the Greek translation of Dan 4:14). A Jewish teacher skilled in sagacious disputation was called an "uprooter of trees." Hence once again the intended meaning is that faith in God's authority is able to effect judgment and salvation and thus is able to accomplish what is humanly impossible.

If one wants to comprehend how the proclamation of Jesus came to be faith in Jesus Christ, it is essential to understand these references. If one compares them with the tradition of faith in the OT and in Judaism, one quickly discovers that not a single other prophet or teacher since the eighth-century prophet Isaiah (cf. Isa 7:9; 28:16; 30:15) spoke of faith as Jesus does here. Into Israel's tradition of faith Jesus introduces a new manner of speaking and thinking about faith. If believers turn to God in prayer and God acts on their behalf, they obtain a share in the activity of almighty God.[29] From the OT all Jews at the time of Jesus know what God's activity denotes; further-

---

[29] On this see Adolf Schlatter, *Der Glaube im Neuen Testament* (6th ed.; Stuttgart: Calwer, 1982) 94–176; Gerhard Ebeling, "Jesus and Faith," *Word and Faith* (trans. James W. Leitch; Philadelphia: Fortress, 1973) 201–46; Hans-Jürgen Hermisson and Eduard Lohse, *Faith* (trans. Douglas W. Stott; Nashville: Abingdon, 1981) 109–12.

more, for them this activity is demonstrated—and that is crucial—through Jesus' word and deed. In the healing narratives to
which I called attention, Jesus works on behalf of humans in
need, as the mediator of the almighty, benevolent God. By con-
demning (the demons of) sickness he establishes God's righteousness that effects salvation.

Thus the question of how the move from the proclamation
of Jesus to faith in Jesus Christ came about has been partly
answered, but not fully. As the mediator of God, Jesus himself
establishes the way to faith in him. Yet in the proclamation of
Jesus "faith" still means quite unequivocally "faith [mediated by
Jesus] in God" (cf. Mark 11:22). Only the account of the healing
of the paralytic alludes to the fact that the men who bring the
paralytic have "faith," that is, confidence in Jesus and in his
healing power (Mark 2:5). In other healing narratives, Jesus
sends away those he healed, for instance, the woman subject to
bleeding in Capernaum, by saying: "Daughter [meaning, as
Luke 13:16 helps to explain, 'daughter of Abraham'], your faith
has made you well; go in peace, and be healed of your disease!"
(Mark 5:34; cf. 10:52 and Luke 7:50). In these cases the orientation of faith is the same; nevertheless it is not yet a developed
faith in Jesus Christ in the sense of post-Easter confessions.

How then does the faith arise that Jesus is the Christ (1 Cor
15:3) or the Son of man, the mediator between the one God and
the humans who need salvation (1 Tim 2:5)? One cannot answer this question definitively without explaining even more
specifically how Jesus' contemporaries thought about Jesus and—
especially—how he viewed himself.

Jesus' Self-designation as "Son of man" and "Messiah"

In his preaching of repentance John the Baptist points to
the "stronger one" who is coming after him, who would baptize
the repentant not only with water, as John does, but with the
Holy Spirit and with fire (cf. Mark 1:7 and Matt 3:11 par. Luke
3:16). In keeping with the OT-Jewish expectation, this "stronger
one" refers to the judge of the world who is to usher in the
judgment and the new creation and, by means of both, the

ultimate kingdom of God. In part the OT identifies the Messiah as a Davidic descendant (cf., e.g., Isa 11:1–9), who is a pioneer of the kingdom of God, and in part it also identifies the Messiah as the heavenly "Son of man" who is to accomplish the everlasting reign of liberty for God's tormented and oppressed people Israel (cf. Dan 7:13–27). Texts subsequent to the OT suggest that the baptizer with Spirit and fire can actually only be the "messianic Son of man" or the "Son of man–Messiah" (cf. 1 Enoch 48:2, 10).[30] Compared to him John the Baptist considers himself unworthy even of the menial slave labor of taking off and putting on sandals (Mark 1:7). Hence John the Baptist's preaching of repentance confronts Jesus with the announcement of the messianic Son of man who is coming to judge and to inaugurate the new creation.

The experience with the Spirit that Jesus receives at his baptism by means of the divine affirmation: "You are my beloved Son; with you I am well pleased" (Mark 1:11), gives him the assurance that he himself is now to carry out in public the work of the Son of man–Messiah announced by the Baptist.[31] In the course of the so-called temptation (Mark 1:12–13), Jesus acknowledges this task. In the "initial decision"[32] he wrestles with the readiness to walk the path of the messianic Son of man in the strict "obedience of sonship" (A. Schlatter) to God's will, and he maintains this decision in Gethsemane, "the concluding decision."[33] Jesus' entire public ministry, from the temptation to its conclusion in the passion, is characterized by this decision: Jesus goes, and wants to go, his way only as the son who is

---

[30] So with Friedrich Lang, "Erwägungen zur eschatologischen Verkündigung Johannes des Täufers," *Jesus Christus in Historie und Theologie: Neutestamentliche Festschrift für Hans Conzelmann zum 60. Geburtstag* (ed. Georg Strecker; Tübingen: J. C. B. Mohr [Paul Siebeck], 1975) 470–71.

[31] Jeremias, *New Testament Theology*, 56, links Mark 1:9–11 par. with Mark 11:27–33 par. and concludes thereby that Jesus perceived his messianic authority to be based on the commission and reception of the Spirit, both of which took place at his baptism.

[32] Cf. Fritz Neugebauer, *Jesu Versuchung: Wegentscheidung am Anfang* (Tübingen: J. C. B. Mohr [Paul Siebeck], 1986).

[33] On the Gethsemane narrative and its historical basis, see Reinhard Feldmeier, *Die Krisis des Gottessohnes* (Tübingen: J. C. B. Mohr [Paul Siebeck], 1987).

obedient to God alone and as the Son of man–Messiah. From a biblical perspective, the three titles of Jesus that occur again and again—"Son of God," "Son of man," and "Messiah"—do not represent alternatives but in a Jewish way[34] they jointly designate Jesus as the one mediator through whom God wills to accomplish his work of redemption, the ultimate establishment of his rule for Israel and for the whole world.

The more recent critical scholarship has repeatedly argued that Jesus himself had not used any of the common Jewish titles ("Son of God," "Messiah," or "Son of man") but instead that the community after Easter gradually attributed them to him. Before Easter Jesus had been no more than, and had at best claimed to be, the final prophetic messenger of God prior to the judgment of the world. Although scholars continue to repeat this viewpoint,[35] it remains an abstraction of research that the texts and historical probability contradict. One makes considerably more progress in the attempt to retrace the rise of faith in Christ by following the text tradition carefully and by realizing that,

---

[34] Schniewind, *Markus*, 193, writes (on Mark 14:62): Everyone was able to "understand [Jesus]: Messiah, Son of God, Son of man, the judge of the world enthroned with God; this was already paralleled in the Jewish tradition. But Jesus says: I am. Precisely because he faces death he is the coming judge of the world; over him is the promise of Isa 52:13; 53:10ff." One can see that Schniewind is correct in this view from the paralleling of various titles for the one mediator of salvation in 4QpsDan ar^a (4Q 246); 11QMelch; 1 Enoch 48–49; 61–62; 4 Ezra 13; etc.

[35] Bultmann, *Theology*, 1:32, observes: "It was soon no longer conceivable that Jesus' life was unmessianic—at least in the circles of Hellenistic Christianity in which the synoptics took form. That Jesus Christ, the Son of God, should have legitimated himself as such even in his earthly activity seemed self-evident, and so the gospel account of his ministry was cast in the light of messianic faith. The contradiction between this point of view and the traditional material finds expression in the theory of the Messiah-secret, which gives the Gospel of Mark its peculiar character. . . ." Käsemann, *Problem*, 43, states: "I consider all passages in which any kind of Messianic prediction occurs to be a kerygma shaped by the community." Bornkamm, *Jesus*, 206–10, argues identically, and Weiss, *Kerygma*, 74, has recently affirmed this view again: ". . . all . . . titles (are) themselves already interpretations by means of which the post-Easter church . . . expressed the eschatological significance of Jesus." Finally Siegfried Schulz, *Neutestamentliche Ethik* (Zurich: Theologischer Verlag, 1987) 32, writes: Jesus "was the last of the prophets, and his appearance and ministry are unique because there is nothing that follows him except God and his kingdom."

given the conspicuous deeds of Jesus and his remarkable message among his contemporaries, the question was inescapable: Who then is this man? What authority—or conversely: what unclean spirit (cf. Mark 3:22, 30)—inspires him? That Jesus would not have answered this question at all (as contemporary critical scholarship has to presuppose) is altogether unlikely and renders the human Jesus a walking historical enigma. In any case, the texts describe him (historically quite credibly) otherwise.

At the outset of his final pilgrimage to Jerusalem, when Jesus briefly retreats with his disciples to the region of Caesarea Philippi, he asks them who the people say he is. They tell him that some say he is John the Baptist (who takes on a new shape in Jesus and his preaching, following his decapitation by Herod Antipas). Others take him to be Elijah, whom God will send, according to Malachi 3:23–24, before the great and dreadful "day of the Lord," in order to "turn the hearts of the fathers to their sons and the hearts of the sons to their fathers" (i.e., to cause them to study afresh the will of God in the form of the Law) and thus keep them from the judgment. Still others hold Jesus to be "one of the prophets," according to the disciples' report (cf. Deut 18:18). The result of all three designations is that one must not eliminate from Jesus' proclamation the call to repentance, urging people to keep the will of God.

Following the disciples' response Jesus continues to ask: " 'But who do you say that I am?' Peter [as representative for all] answered him, 'You are the Christ.' And he [Jesus] charged them to tell no one about him. And he began to teach them that the Son of man must suffer many things, and be rejected by the elders and the chief priests and the scribes, and be killed, and after three days rise again. And he said this plainly" (Mark 8:29–32, RSV). According to this report (repeated in Matthew and Luke), Jesus certainly discusses his mission with his disciples in the secluded place. Jesus essentially affirms the emerging realization among the disciples that he is the Messiah; finally before the Jewish court and before Pilate he indeed confesses himself to be the messianic Son of God (cf. Mark 14:62; 15:2).

But he quickly enjoins his disciples to withhold their insight from the public for the time being. The likely reason for this secrecy is that the public proclamation "Jesus is the Messiah!" would threaten Jesus' pilgrimage and mission, which the people would perceive too rigidly in line with their vivid expectation that the Messiah from the family of David would free Israel from Roman domination, purge Jerusalem from the godless heathens, and usher in the era of righteousness (cf. Pss. Sol. 17:21–46). Jesus does not want to be made to fit this mold. Not until matters in Jerusalem finally reach their decisive point does Jesus openly confess his messianic mission in front of his Jewish judges and the Roman prefect. Even then, however, he brings it into the context of his task of serving God as the "Son of man" (cf. Mark 14:61–62 par.).

Following Daniel 7, the Enoch tradition (1 Enoch 40; 45–49; 53; 61–62; 71), and 4 Ezra 13, the Son of man is a messianic figure. Like the Davidic Messiah, the Son of man is expected to execute the final judgment on behalf of God, to establish God's rule for Israel, as well as to gather God's eschatological people of righteousness. Yet the national political coloring of the expectation of the Davidic Messiah recedes noticeably in the Son of man texts. Jesus adopts the mysterious Son of man title, rare in the Jewish tradition, from the preaching of John the Baptist and, in the course of his ministry, puts his own unique imprint upon it:[36] During his earthly life Jesus wants to unite God, his Father, afresh with Israel by means of his kind devotion to the "poor" (cf. Isa 61:1–2), his serving love (Luke 19:10; Mark 10:42–45; John 13:2–17), and his vicarious suffering. It is only after this earthly venue of service that Jesus expects his exaltation to the right hand of God and his inauguration into the eschatological judgeship (Mark 14:61–62

---

[36]Cf. Werner Georg Kümmel, "Jesus—der Menschensohn?" *SbWGF* 20 (3, 1984) 179: "Jesus adopted the Jewish-apocalyptic expectation of the eschatological 'human' as judge and ruler, but correlated it in a way unprecedented in the Jewish conceptual world—with his person and ministry in the present —and thus radically reshaped it." Although Kümmel does not consider the notion of the vicarious atonement "to be reconciled with Jesus' salvific proclamation" (178), for good reasons Traugott Holtz, *Jesus aus Nazareth* (Berlin and Leipzig: Union, 1979) 73, argues the very opposite on the basis of the texts: "Jesus [perceived] himself in a manner that his path to the eschatological Son of man could only take him through suffering."

par.; Luke 12:8–9 par.). For precisely this reason he places Peter's messianic expectation (and that of all his disciples) in the light of his mission: to enter into suffering first as messianic Son of man, and only through suffering to enter into the glory and power of the resurrection (Mark 8:27–33 par.).

Because the early Jewish tradition had no tradition of a suffering Messiah except for Zechariah 12:10; 13:7 (cf. Matt 24:30; Mark 14:27 par.), and because the OT–Jewish texts do not mention a destiny of suffering for the Son of man either, Jesus' response to Peter's messianic confession is quite unprecedented. Here one confronts a revolutionizing new interpretation, born out of Jesus' proximity to God and out of his obedience as Son, of the entire Jewish expectation of the Son of man and of the Messiah. If Jesus' self-designation as "Son of man" was already enigmatic, this new version of the Son of man title is all the more a mystery. Thus Jesus' response to Peter's confession encounters resistance and a lack of understanding. Mark 8:32–33 says: "And Peter took him [Jesus], and began to rebuke him. But turning and seeing his disciples, he rebuked Peter, and said, 'Get behind me, Satan! For you are not on the side of God, but of humans.' " This uncommonly sharp (and therefore not possibly only post-Easter) word of Jesus sternly puts Peter in his place of discipleship behind Jesus; by means of his resistance to his Lord's willingness to suffer, Peter as tempter opposes Jesus.

After all this, Jesus' earthly ministry as messianic Son of man is shrouded in mystery even for the disciples themselves. The so-called messianic secret,[37] which occurs repeatedly in Mark's Gospel (particularly clearly in 9:9–10), is not merely a post-Easter theological construct, and it has nothing to do with an attempt after Easter to obscure the fact that Jesus' life took its course unmessianically and has been placed in the light of

---

[37] Wilhelm Wrede, *The Messianic Secret* (trans. J. C. S. Greig; London: James Clarke, 1971), has interpreted the messianic secret as a Christian theory given by the tradition to Mark the evangelist. Bultmann, *Theology*, 1:32, interpreted it in the sense of a veiling of the unmessianic life of Jesus. But Heikki Räisänen, *The 'Messianic Secret' in Mark* (trans. C. Tuckett; Edinburgh: T. & T. Clark, 1990), has shown that Mark the evangelist is working with a multilayered tradition and not (with Wrede) one that can be interpreted in only one direction. The Markan "theory" has pre-Easter roots.

messianism only from the perspective of Easter. Rather, this secrecy has to do with a fundamental feature of the ministry of Jesus himself. His proclamation in parables and signs (symbolic actions) could be and should be intelligible only to those who are truly open to them; to the outsiders their meaning remains hidden and, in part, is even offensive (cf. Mark 4:33–34). It is by no means accidental that Jesus' exclamation of salvation and jubilation in Matthew 11:25–30 begins : "I thank you, Father, Lord of heaven and earth, that you have hidden these things [that which I am proclaiming] from the wise and the understanding and revealed them to the simple. Yes, Father, such was your gracious will" (Matt 11:25–26). Even for Jesus' closest companions, his path, as Son of the Father, is always a mystery; they continually construe his actions incorrectly (cf. Mark 1:36–38; 8:32–33; 10:35ff.; Luke 9:54–56; 24:21). Only after Christ appears in new, divine life to the disciples, all of whom had deserted him on the night of the betrayal (Mark 14:50 par.), and after, in the power of the Spirit, they learn to confess Jesus' resurrection and exaltation to the right hand of God, only then do they truly know what earthly Lord they have followed. In the final analysis, who Jesus was and who he is remains hidden without the Spirit of faith (cf. John 14:16, 26; 15:26; 16:12–14).

But to return to the topic, one should hold on to what the account of Mark 8:27–33 offers in posing the question. The Markan text has the two titles, fundamental to the early post-Easter confessions: "Christ" (i.e., "Messiah"; cf. 1 Cor 15:3) and "Son of man." (I show later that this title is behind the "man" in 1 Tim 2:5.) That Jesus himself openly attests to his messianic mission before the Jewish court and before Pilate is documented in Mark 14:62 par.; 15:2 par., including the inscription on the cross formulated by the Romans (not by Christians): "The King of the Jews" (Mark 15:26).

Thus I have traced the titles of Jesus that Christians have adopted from the Easter confession. They obviously originated in the pre-Easter Jesus tradition and were affirmed and used by Jesus himself. To attribute these titles only to the post-Easter insight and to the faith of the community would mean to make Jesus' path, including his passion, historically incomprehensible.

Understanding the Passion of Jesus

One has to investigate the meaning of the passion more thoroughly for three reasons. First, I have noted the striking peculiarity of Jesus' predictions of the passion. Second, I have mentioned that Jesus' messianic call to repentance has its underside: the unrepentant face the judgment. Third, the two biblical confessions of Christ, with which I began as models, thematically refer precisely to Jesus' vicarious suffering. Hence the question is unavoidable: Why did Jesus have to and want to take the way of suffering as Son of man–Messiah sent by God?

In order to penetrate the mystery of Jesus' passion one must link the given historical perspectives with the attempt to ponder (with understanding) Jesus' own willingness to suffer.

The Historical Necessity of the Passion[38]

If one keeps in mind Jesus' way from Galilee to Jerusalem according to the first three Gospels, one quickly discovers that this way is marked by an increasingly intensifying confrontation with representatives of all the important Jewish religious parties of his time. Whereas his disciples follow him almost unconditionally and put their hopes in him, and whereas he is continually surrounded by the poor and the needy, Jesus' call to repentance and his proclamation of the kingdom of God in parables, dialogues, and messianic symbolic actions (i.e., table fellowship with the poor and the rejected, as well as miracles of healing) represent a challenge that becomes increasingly unbearable for many Pharisees, Zealots, and rich Jews. But the most powerful opposition to Jesus emerges from the party of the high priests and of the Sadducean nobility that leads Jerusalem. They dominate and administer the temple; by his demonstrative act of cleansing the temple in the last few days of his ministry, Jesus provoked especially them.

---

[38] On this section see ch. 2, "Why Did Jesus Have to Die?"

In all probability one should understand the cleansing of the temple as a messianic symbolic action of Jesus.[39] At the dawn of the kingdom of God Israel expected the exaltation of "the mountain with the house of the Lord"—Zion—to become the mountain of the world (Mic 4:1ff.; Isa 2:1–5). Various early Jewish texts refer to the glorification and the new building of the temple in that eschatological time.[40] The Essenes of Qumran expect the Messiah from the clan of David to rebuild the sanctuary (cf. 4QFlor 1:1ff.). The early pharisaic Psalms of Solomon speak of the same Davidic Messiah: "he will glorify the Lord at a place towering above the whole earth and will cleanse Jerusalem by sanctification, as it was in the beginning" (Pss. Sol. 17:30; cf. Mic 4:1ff.). Book 5 of the so-called Sibylline Oracles (414–33) speaks of "a blessed man from the ends of the heavens," likely the messianic Son of man, who will gloriously renew the city of God and the temple. In the Targum (i.e., the Aramaic paraphrase) of Isaiah 53 from the post-NT era the Messiah will reestablish the temple, which is unclean and given over to be destroyed (in AD 70).

Therefore, by means of his action against the money changers and sellers of sacrificial animals in the temple, tersely described in Mark 11:15–17, Jesus is clearly within the messianic horizon of expectation. If by his action he speaks—which is very likely—about the destruction and rebuilding of the temple by himself (cf. John 2:19), the meaning of the symbolic act be-

---

[39] Very aptly by Pokorný, *Genesis of Christology*, 47–48: "Some of Jesus' deeds are to be interpreted as prophetic symbolic actions. . . . They are differentiated from prophetic actions in that they give expression to eschatological fulfillment. Such an action is the cleansing of the temple (Mark 11:15f.). . . . Through his symbolic action Jesus proclaimed the fulfillment of the promise about the pilgrimage of the people toward Zion (Isa 56:7, among other passages), which he perhaps interpreted in the light of the expectation of a new eschatological temple. . . . It was perhaps on this or on a similar occasion that he uttered a *vaticinium* about the destruction of the temple by way of a prophetic threat, which the evangelist later modified *ex eventu* (Mark 13:2). This was clearly also the immediate occasion of the accusation against Jesus before the Sanhedrin." In my opinion one has to give greater emphasis than Pokorný does to the fact that Jesus' procedure in the temple is messianically motivated.

[40] Sanders, *Jesus and Judaism*, 77–90, cites and discusses critically the relevant references.

comes clear: Jesus presses for a decision between the traditional cult and the presence of God that he himself, the messianic Son of man, proclaimed and mediated.[41] Only by this means can the temple again become a house of prayer for all nations (cf. Isa 56:7).

One would expect the Sadducees to consider Jesus' action as a threat to the institution of the temple and to take appropriate measures against Jesus, and Jesus makes allowance for such action. This is indicated in the parable of the Wicked Tenants in Mark 12:1–12 par., which Jesus tells shortly after the cleansing of the temple and again aims at the Sadducees. Jesus goes for it all in his final appearance in Jerusalem.

If one takes cumulatively all those who offended at Jesus' appearance, there arises an overwhelming column of enemies to whom Jesus ultimately falls prey. From a historical perspective, it is unavoidable that Jesus and his opponents are on a collision course and that in Jerusalem they finally put him on trial as a messianic false prophet who violated Israel's regulation of faith and cult and as one who led people astray into heresy (cf. Deut 13:2–7; 17:1–7; 18:20).[42]

---

[41] Helmut Merklein, *Jesu Botschaft von der Gottesherrschaft* (SBS III; Stuttgart: Katholisches Bibelwerk, 1983) 135–36, takes a similar view: "The problem for him [Jesus] was probably not the cult as a God-ordained order, but—similarly to the case of the conflict about the Torah—the manner in which *Israel* used this cult for themselves. If Israel is one single collective of calamity, whose only possibility for salvation consists of accepting God's eschatological act of election, represented by Jesus, they cannot claim the cult as a possibility of atonement *against* God's act of election that eradicates sin, nor can they excuse themselves, by appealing to a cultic possibility for salvation, from the decision *for* the act of election to be appropriated. This decision may have been Jesus' concern in his provocative words and deed in the temple." Also instructive on the temple cleansing is B. F. Meyer, *The Aims of Jesus* (London: SCM, 1979) 197–202.

[42] Cf. Hengel, *Charismatic Leader*, 45ff.; August Strobel, *Die Stunde der Wahrheit: Untersuchungen zum Strafverfahren gegen Jesus* (WUNT 21; Tübingen: J. C. B. Mohr [Paul Siebeck], 1980) 81ff.; Otto Betz, *Probleme des Prozesses Jesu* (*ANRW* II/25.1; Berlin and New York: de Gruyter, 1982) 577ff., 638–39. In *Wer war schuld an Jesu Tod?* Lapide begins his critique of the reports of the Gospels concerning the Jewish proceedings against Jesus with historical perspectives and theses that have long been corrected and refuted by the authors mentioned.

Remarkably Jesus does not withdraw from this conflict by escaping the scene. Rather, before the Jewish court he explicitly confesses to his mission and boldly adds that the day would be coming when his present human judges had to answer to him as the Son of man–judge of the world who will be sitting on God's throne of judgment and who will be coming with the clouds of heaven. To the high priest's question: "Are you the Messiah, the Son of the Blessed?" Jesus answers: "I am; and you will see the Son of man seated at the right hand of Power, and coming with the clouds of heaven" (Mark 14:61–62 par.).[43] The claim to be Messiah is not itself blasphemy yet; but at the same time to exalt oneself to be the judge of the world at the right hand of God and to announce the judgment of the leading judges of Israel—that indeed is presumption of divine authority and hence blasphemy, incurring death according to Jewish law (cf. Exod 22:27; Lev 24:15–16; John 19:7).[44]

Thus Jesus is charged with messianic agitation and divine presumption. Because the Jewish court is not allowed to carry out a death sentence at the time of Jesus (cf. John 19:31), his Sadducean opponents must denounce Jesus as a messianic in-surrectionist before Pilate the following morning and thereby

---

[43] In every new edition (to date) of the *Arbeitsbuch zum Neuen Testament* by Hans Conzelmann and Andreas Lindemann ET *Interpreting the New Testament: An Introduction to the Principles and Methods of N.T. Exegesis* (trans. Siegfried Schatzmann; Peabody, Mass: Hendrickson, 1988), based on the 8th rev. German ed., 1985), the assertion is made with regard to Mark 14:61–62 that "this scene is devoid of a historical core, for the presentation of the trial is altogether determined christologically. The reference of Mark 14:61f. was very obviously drawn up as a compendium of the community's Christology; it is intended to show that all of the messianic titles—Messiah, Son of God, Son of man—are of equal value" (323–24). This assessment ignores not only the cumulative use of titles in early Jewish texts (see n. 34 above), but also the linguistic relationship of the passage with 4QpsDan ar[a] (4Q 246), which points to an ancient tradition, and the new analysis of the trial of Jesus presented by Strobel, *Stunde*. Consequently Strobel argues differently on Mark 14:61–62: "In its core we are confronted with a unique tradition, whose likely highly factual content is Jesus' own expectation of exaltation, voiced before the highest court of the Jewish people during this Passover period. The issue here is the historical core of the expectation and mission of Jesus."

[44] Cf. Strobel, *Stunde*, 92ff.; Betz, *Probleme*, 636ff.; and Otfried Hofius, "βλασφημία," *EDNT*, 1:220–21.

urge the Roman prefect to take action against the suspect. Jesus also maintains his messianic confession before Pilate and does not attempt to defend himself (Mark 15:1–5). His confession earns him a scourging and death on the cross. Thus Jesus faces death with purpose and cognizance.

Jesus' Readiness to Offer Himself

Jesus clearly does not escape from the impending fate because all his deeds, including the cleansing of the temple and the confession before the Jewish court, correspond with the divine mission as Son of man–Messiah, received at baptism, and for one last and decisive time Jesus wants to confront the people of God who had gathered for the Passover festival with his message.[45] Jesus is less concerned with protecting his own life than with his task to bring to bear the affirmation and claim of the one God who is present, whom he calls his "Father." One can recognize from the temptation at the outset of his path and from the conflict in prayer in Gethsemane at his path's conclusion that the fulfillment of this mission does not fall into his lap. Although he represents God, Jesus is also a human being with flesh and blood; and it cost him prayer, fasting, sweat, and tears to struggle through to the perfect obedience in which he walks (cf. Heb 5:7–10). Classical evidence for Jesus' readiness to offer himself is found in the word about the ransom in Mark 10:45, spoken in the context of the departure for Jerusalem, and also in the words of institution at the Lord's Supper in Mark 14:22–25 par. In both instances Jesus applies the traditions of the ransom and of the suffering servant of God (Isa 53) to himself and to his path.

A comparison of both texts makes it evident that the saying concerning the ransom[46] has been incorporated in the

---

[45] "We may, however, assume that first and foremost his journey to Jerusalem was undertaken in order to confront the people in the holy city with the message of the kingdom of God and to summon them at the eleventh hour to make their decision," Bornkamm, *Jesus*, 155.

[46] Cf. my essay, "Vicariously Giving His Life for Many, Mark 10:45 (Matt. 20:28)," *Reconciliation, Law, and Righteousness* (trans. Everett Kalin; Philadelphia: Fortress, 1986) 16–29, and the substantiation there for the following arguments.

formulation of the confession of 1 Timothy 2:5–6, which I have already discussed. The community reiterates as confession what they have heard concerning Jesus. The logion says: "The Son of man also came not to be served but to serve, and to give his life as a ransom for many" (Mark 10:45 and Matt 20:28). This saying presents a self-interpretation of Jesus' mission that is conceived and formulated entirely from the perspective of the OT. As the Son of man he is not here to demand and receive on earth the service and homage that the heavenly Son of man is due from the angels of God and the nations of the world, according to Daniel 7:13–14. The converse is the case. He is sent and in the name and on behalf of God is here to serve "the many" whose life is forfeited through sin and guilt before God, and indeed to serve to the point of offering up his body and life as a ransom for all. The backdrop of this saying is found in the announcements of (the so-called Second) Isaiah, in Isaiah 43:3–4 and 53:11–12. According to Isaiah 43:3–4 God himself, as the savior of Israel, purposes to pay the ransom out of love for his guilt-ridden people, a ransom redeeming this people in the form of a "human" whom he offers up for Israel's salvation.[47] Isaiah 53:11–12 says: "My servant, the righteous one, will justify the many; among the great and with the mighty he will divide the spoil, because he poured out his life unto death and was numbered with the transgressors. For he bore the sins of many and made intercession for the guilty."

Isaiah 53 directs us further toward the two sayings in which Jesus, during his farewell meal with the Twelve and with all those represented by the circle of the Twelve, consoles them unreservedly in his existence on their behalf: "This is my body" and "this is my blood of the covenant, which is poured out for many" (Mark 14:22, 24).[48] In these two statements Jesus grants

---

[47] Although the MT of Isa 43:4a speaks of God who will give *'ādām*, "human being(s)," for Israel, 1QIsa[a] reads *hā-'ādām*. Grammatically this surely refers to an article to determine the class (cf. GKC, §126*l*), though of course one may also read: "the human being (in general)," and then interpret this with reference to the Son of man.

[48] Details on the words of institution are found in ch. 3, "The New Testament Witness Concerning the Lord's Supper."

those participating in the meal a share in the fruit of his vicarious death and causes them to be partakers in the new covenant and candidates for the messianic table fellowship in God's consummate kingdom (cf. Mark 14:25 with Isa 25:6ff.). As strange as the situation might be, given contemporary standards of thought, the wording, pointed out in the texts indicated, is clear: Jesus is willing to undertake his earthly pilgrimage as Son of man, and is ultimately able to stand his ground, only because he understands himself to be God's servant and the ransom, in person, chosen by God as the existential representative of Israel and of all the lost. To formulate it in modern terms: Jesus lived and suffered as the propitiator (reconciler) of God with the sinners of Israel and of the whole world; or, more succinctly still: Jesus lived and suffered as the embodiment of God's loving will to forgive sins.

The Experience of Easter Leading to the Confession of Faith and Faith in Jesus Christ

In keeping with 1 Corinthians 15:3–5 and 1 Timothy 2:5–6, the early Christian confessions of Jesus as the Christ and mediator of God are confessions looking back on the fulfilled mission and passion of Jesus from the Easter perspective and praising him as the exalted Lord whom God had raised. Without the Easter events these confessions would never have come about, despite the proclamation of Jesus. The Easter events are constitutive for these confessions, and for the Christian confession of Jesus Christ in general, for the simple reason that only the Easter event gave the disciples of Jesus the assurance that Jesus' sacrifice had not been in vain. In order to conclude, I need to clarify this point now.

As the night of Good Friday falls over Jesus, who died on the tree of ignominy and whom friends hurriedly laid in a rocky tomb, every Jew opposed to Jesus could—indeed had—to say with Deuteronomy 21:22–23: This one who has been hung on the cross has suffered his just punishment; he died "cursed of God!" His disciples, gripped by fear and doubt, are able to recover from this logical and dreadful interpretation of Jesus' death on the cross (cf. John 19:31; Acts 5:30; 10:39; Justin, Dialogue with Trypho 89:2; 90:1) only when the crucified one appears to them in divine life on Easter morning, after they have become convinced by the report of some women from Jesus' circle that his tomb outside the city had been found opened and empty on Easter morning. When the same Lord, whom they all had eventually deserted on the night of the betrayal (cf. Mark 14:50), appears to his disciples in new divine life in Galilee and Jerusalem and greets them with: "Peace be with you!" (cf. Luke 24:36; John 20:19, 21, 26), Peter and the other disciples who are present learn and recognize that God has not rejected their Lord but has vindicated him. By means of the greeting of peace the living Son of God receives them afresh into the fellowship that they had renounced for fear of their life. They receive forgiveness for their failure and their desertion. A few years later Paul, the persecutor of Christians, has a similar experience outside Damascus.

This is not the place to analyze in detail the NT narratives and brief accounts of Jesus' appearances to Peter, the Twelve, Mary Magdalene, and the disciples of Emmaus, and, encompassing these, the narratives of the discovery of Jesus' empty tomb on Easter morning. Nevertheless, I need to point out emphatically that neither the appearance accounts nor the stories of the tomb can be dismissed as merely apologetic legends. The appearance accounts reflect genuine, religious, fundamental experiences of the new and fresh encounter with the glorified Jesus after Good Friday. To deny them, as Ferdinand Christian Baur already perceived,[49] would render inexplicable the development of early Christianity and its mission. The narratives of Jesus' empty tomb likewise emerge as apologetic legends only in our late Gentile Christian perspective. Originally they certainly did not render facile the proclamation of Jesus' salvific death and God's authentication among the Jews (of Jerusalem), and precisely this circumstance proves them to be ancient tradition. In Israel some martyred prophets were called upon as living, heavenly interces-

---

[49] See Klaus Scholder, "Ferdinand Christian Baur als Historiker," *EvT* 21 (1961) 455–56.

sors at the time of Jesus, while their mortal remains rested (incorruptibly) in the grave until the day of judgment.[50] The stories of the discovery of the empty tomb demonstrate that the Christians were not able to follow this Jewish form of piety with reference to Jesus; they would not and could not see and proclaim Jesus as the martyred prophet that modern scholarship would like to see in Jesus. The Son of man whom God raised is not to be sought among the dead (Luke 24:5); already now he has been exalted at the right hand of God bodily. For him and in him God's eschatological resurrection of the dead has already become reality filled with hope (cf. 1 Cor 15:4, 20ff.; Rom 1:4). The cross of Jesus is not merely a horrid tool of martyrdom; rather the issue of Calvary is "a coming to God by passing through the sentence of death,"[51] opened up for all sinners by Jesus—the life-giving atonement and the promised overcoming of the death that gripped the world when Adam was driven out of paradise.

CONCLUSION

Adopting the Baptist's call to repentance in his own way, Jesus called for faith in the gospel of the approaching kingdom of God that he himself proclaimed (cf. Mark 1:15), and he spoke of "faith in God" (Mark 11:22) in an altogether new way. The Easter witnesses adopted the gospel of Jesus, as well as the faith in God he taught, and incorporated them into the gospel of Jesus Christ that they proclaimed to Jews and Gentiles as the message of salvation.[52] In the missionary proclamation, faith from now on means faith in the God who fulfilled his promised work of salvation concerning Israel and the world through the mission, the atoning death, and the resurrection of Jesus (Rom 4:24–25). For those who confess Jesus as the one who atones and as Lord, salvation from the approaching final judgment is guar-

---

[50] Cf. Joachim Jeremias, *Heiligengräber in Jesu Umwelt* (1958) 126ff.

[51] Hartmut Gese, "The Atonement," *Essays on Biblical Theology* (trans. Keith Crim; Minneapolis: Augsburg, 1981) 114.

[52] On the continuity of the proclamation of the Gospel, see my article, "Evangelium," *EKL*, 2d ed., 1:1217–21.

anteed in Jesus, the crucified Lord and Messiah who was raised from the dead and is exalted at the right hand of God (Acts 2:36). Precisely for this reason Paul, by adopting Christian confessional traditions, could state: "if you confess with your lips that Jesus is Lord and believe in your heart that God raised him from the dead, you will be saved" (Rom 10:9). Although Jesus called for faith, mediated by himself, in the one God who is able to do all things, his passion and resurrection resulted in faith in Jesus Christ. Through him the almighty God allotted to his chosen people Israel and to the gentile world the righteousness that they need to live with and before God. The believers in the ancient world were recognized as "Christians" (Acts 11:26) on account of this faith and of belonging to Christ, and they continue to be recognized as such.

If one takes a backward glance, Jesus of Nazareth indeed appears as the Christ of faith, as Schlatter argued. The decisive impulses for faith and confession of him as Messiah (Christ) and Son of man have their starting point in his earthly ministry and word, in Easter, and in the witness tradition of the OT, through which Jesus' ministry and God's redemptive deed actually become intelligible. Already before Easter Jesus was a controversial and persecuted individual; he remains controversial in the (post-)Easter perspective as well. He can be and will be truly understood only by those who intently engage Jesus' message (cf. John 7:16–17) and for whom God opens up faith through Jesus' message.

2

WHY DID JESUS HAVE TO DIE?[1]

DIFFICULTIES OF RESPONSE

HOWEVER OBVIOUS THE QUESTION OF THE REASON AND PURPOSE of Jesus' death might be for friends and critics of Christianity, it is difficult to answer it clearly and intelligibly. The theological interpretation of the cross and resurrection of Jesus has concerned theology since the days of early Christianity, and Paul knew very well why his confidence was in the wisdom of faith alone to penetrate the offense of the cross of Jesus comprehensibly (cf. 1 Cor 1:18–2:16). Thus if the problem is already complex with regard to the NT itself, theologians and prospective pastors of the twentieth century need to be further aware of particular difficulties in comprehension in the context of addressing the topic question. These difficulties are related to the history of research and of ideas.

In view of contemporary Gospel criticism, it seems impossible simply to refer back to the accounts of the Synoptics or of

---

[1] In the original German form this was a guest lecture, given in Lund on September 27, 1984; it has been supplemented for publication.

the Gospel of John to answer this question. Especially the statements of Jesus concerning his own death and the passion narrative on the whole are today almost universally suspected to
have originated only in the reflective faith of the (late) post-Easter community. Even the apostolic letters do not seem to lend
themselves to much progress. For instance, modernity's enlightened consciousness perceives the answer given several times by
the apostle Paul: Jesus died to atone for our sins (cf. 1 Cor
15:3–5; 2 Cor 5:21; Gal 1:4; 2:20; Rom 3:25–26; 8:3–4 etc.), as
religiously unworthy and unacceptable. A God who needs the
blood sacrifice of his own Son in order to be merciful to sinners
impresses the modern human as an idol that has nothing to do
(nor is allowed to have anything to do) with the spirit of Christianity. A deep-rooted skepticism toward the Catholic doctrine
of the Mass (modified at important points since the sixteenth
century)[2] among the Reformed churches lends additional importance to this enlightened criticism regarding the apparently
unreasonably primitive christological notion of sacrifice.[3] Under these circumstances one is not surprised that the question
tends to remain open or is answered only by means of careful
circumscriptions in theology. This situation in the discussion,
however, does not absolve theologians, pastors, and teachers of
religion from their obligation to answer as clearly as possible the
question of the purpose of Jesus' death vis-à-vis their students,
communities, and pupils.

  In my attempt to formulate an answer, I begin with two
presuppositions in terms of methodology and of the history of
research: (1) Despite all the (justified) criticism on the limita-

---

  [2] The contemporary Catholic dictum is: "The sacrifice of the Mass is a
sacramental *representation, remembrance,* and *gift* [German *Vergegenwärtigung,
Gedächtnis, Zuwendung*] of the sacrifice of the cross. . . . Hence the Eucharist is
not a new and independent sacrifice replacing the sacrifice of the cross or even
merely supplementing it. It is the sacramental bringing into the present of the
sacrifice on the cross procured once for all," *Katholischer Erwachsenen-Kate-
chismus* (ed. Deutsche Bischofskonferenz, 1985) 354.

  [3] On the history of the enlightened (and confessional) criticism of the NT
notion of the (atoning) sacrifice, cf. Ulrich Wilckens's most instructive *Der Brief
an die Römer* (EKKNT; Zurich: Benziger; Neukirchen-Vluyn: Neukirchener,
1978) 1:233–43.

tions of the historical method, I still contend that it is possible and theologically essential to penetrate the events and experiences of the biblical era by means of historical research, and to reconstruct it with understanding. (2) Together with friends and colleagues (among whom B. Gerhardsson, M. Hengel, H. Schürmann, and R. Riesner deserve particular mention), I have become convinced in recent years that the synoptic tradition is developed from a carefully controlled continuity of tradition, growing from the period of Jesus into the postapostolic era.[4] Hence I consider it imperative to treat the kerygmatic gospel tradition as historically reliable wherever no compelling historical reasons militate against it.[5] This point also applies to the

---

[4] See Birger Gerhardsson, *Memory and Manuscript* (Lund: Gleerup, 1961); critically continued in idem, *The Origins of the Gospel Traditions* (Philadelphia: Fortress, 1977); idem, "The Path of the Gospel Tradition," *The Gospel and the Gospels* (ed. Peter Stuhlmacher; Grand Rapids: Eerdmans, 1991) 75–96; idem, *The Gospel Tradition* (ConBNT 15; Lund: Gleerup, 1986); Martin Hengel, "Jesus als messianischer Lehrer der Weisheit und die Anfänge der Christologie," *Sagesse et Religion* (Colloque de Strasbourg; Paris: Presses universitaires de France, 1979) 148–88; idem, "Literary, Theological, and Historical Problems in the Gospel of Mark," *The Gospel and the Gospels*, 209–51; idem, "The Gospel of Mark: Time of Origin and Situation," *Studies in the Gospel of Mark* (trans. John Bowden; Philadelphia: Fortress, 1985) 1–30; Heinz Schürmann, "Die vorösterlichen Anfänge der Logientradition," *Traditionsgeschichtliche Untersuchungen zu den synoptischen Evangelien* (Düsseldorf: Patmos, 1968) 39–64; Rainer Riesner, *Jesus als Lehrer* (WUNT 2/7, 2d ed.; Tübingen: J. C. B. Mohr [Paul Siebeck], 1984); idem, "Der Ursprung der Jesus-Überlieferung," *TZ* 38 (1982) 495–513. On the controls of the tradition, see James Dunn, "Prophetic 'I'-Sayings and the Jesus-Tradition: The Importance of Testing Prophetic Utterances within Early Christianity," (*NTS* 24 1977/78) 175–98. David Aune closes the paragraph on "Christian Prophets and the Sayings of Jesus" in his profound book, *Prophecy in Early Christianity and the Ancient Mediterranean World* (Grand Rapids: Eerdmans, 1983), by saying: "German NT scholars, it appears, have seized the hypothesis of the creative role of Christian prophets because it both accounts for the additions to the sayings tradition and absolves the early Christians from any culpability in the forging of inauthentic words of Jesus. In spite of the theological attractiveness of the theory, however, the historical evidence in support of the theory lies largely in the creative imagination of scholars" (p. 245).

[5] So already Oscar Cullmann, *Salvation in History* (trans. Sidney G. Sowers, et al.; London: SCM, 1967) 192. I want to point out emphatically that the position taken above does not imply the end of the historical-critical investigation of all four Gospels. On the synchronic level (of the text) all four Gospels are post-Easter witnesses of history and faith that one can probe

essential sayings of Jesus concerning his death and to the passion narrative. From these presuppositions—which continue to
be subject to discussion—arise the following historical and
theological perspectives.

REASONS FOR JESUS' CONDEMNATION

When one focuses upon Jesus and his ministry, as the three
Synoptic Gospels account for it, the severity of Jesus' death on
the cross is certainly not concealed. Mark says:

> At three o'clock Jesus cried out with a loud voice, "Eloi, Eloi,
> lema sabachthani?" which means, "My God, my God, why have
> you forsaken me?" [Ps 22:2]. When some of the bystanders
> heard it, they said, "Listen, he is calling for Elijah." And someone
> ran, filled a sponge with sour wine, put it on a stick, and gave it
> to him to drink, saying, "Wait, let us see whether Elijah will
> come to take him down." Then Jesus gave a loud cry and
> breathed his last (Mark 15:34–37, NRSV).

Jesus' dying in this manner confronts Christians and non-
Christians with the question: Why did Jesus have to die? From
the very beginning the answers were contrasted. Jesus' most
influential Jewish opponents replied: "This man had to die
because a religious deceiver and false prophet must be elimi-
nated from the context of the people of Israel, according to the
law of Moses" (cf. Deut 13; 17:1–7; 18:20).[6] Pilate, the repre-

---

historically (within the realm of the possible) only by careful diachronic analysis of the tradition. The only problem with this (indispensable, in my opinion)
diachronic analysis is that the criteria of form criticism, itself critical of tradition, have meanwhile proved too flawed to construct reliable historical evalua-
tions of what is historically primary or secondary, Palestinian or (only)
Hellenistic, a saying of Jesus or prophetic (community) construction. Eduard
Lohse ignores all of this in his essay, "Jesu Worte im Zeugnis seiner Gemeinde,"
TLZ 112 (1987) 705–16, and merely summarizes the outdated state of affairs in
the investigation, as delineated by the authors mentioned in n. 4. On this issue,
see also my essay, "The Theme: The Gospel and the Gospels," *The Gospel and
the Gospels*, 1–25, esp. 6–8. From the perspective of the history of research, one
certainly welcomes with good reasons Klaus Berger's attempt to base the history
of the form of the NT on the premise of literary investigation. Cf. his *Form-
geschichte des Neuen Testaments* (Heidelberg: Quelle and Meyer, 1984).

   [6] In *Die Stunde der Wahrheit* (WUNT 21; Tübingen: J. C. B. Mohr [Paul

sentative of the Roman occupation forces in Palestine at the time of Jesus, responded: "This Jesus of Nazareth had to be crucified to serve as a shock treatment, so that henceforth no one else will dare to assert himself as the messianic king of Israel in the purview of the Romans, and incite the Jewish people to rebellion."[7] Since Easter, however, the disciples of Jesus answered: "Jesus our Lord . . . was put to death [by God] for our trespasses and raised for our justification" (Rom 4:24–25). How could such diverse answers come about?

The response of the Jewish opponents of Jesus is quite understandable. During his ministry in Galilee and Judea Jesus did little to endear himself to Pharisees, scribes, rich Jews, Zealots, or even to priests and Sadducees. On the contrary, he offended and challenged all of them with his unfamiliar words and deeds. One need only recall the following six scenes.

First incident: Instead of keeping with good pharisaic tradition by caring for the weak and the sick on a weekday and refraining from all assistance on the Sabbath, Jesus provocatively heals precisely on a holy day and, more than that, declares himself to be the Lord of the Sabbath (cf. Mark 2:28; 3:1ff.). It is not surprising that this conduct offends Pharisees.

Second scene: No less for every pious Jew than for us today it was a matter of course to avoid the society of notorious sinners and of shady business dealers. What does Jesus do instead? In his message he addresses "tax gatherers and sinners"

Siebeck], 1980), August Strobel demonstrated that the reproof voiced against Jesus—that he had been a *planos*, a deceiver, beginning with Matt 27:63 until Justin's *Dialogue with Trypho* (69:7; 108:1)—is to be seen against the background of Deut 13; 17:12; and 18:20 (and the early Jewish legal traditions originating from these texts). They represent the historical reason for Jesus' arrest and condemnation by the Sanhedrin. Under these circumstances the Markan presentation of the passion deserves much more historical confidence than scholars have afforded it thus far (cf. Strobel, 4). On the reproof of Jesus being a religious imposter, see also Otto Betz, *Probleme des Prozesses Jesu* (*ANRW* II/25.1; Berlin and New York: de Gruyter, 1982) 577ff., 594ff., as well as Graham N. Stanton, "Aspects of Early Christian-Jewish Polemic and Apologetic," *NTS* 31 (1985) 377–92.

[7] This is the meaning of the warning and deterrent of the so-called *titulus* on the cross, as formulated by the Romans, not by the Christians (Mark 14:26 par.). On its historical and christological meaning, see Niels Alstrup Dahl, *The Crucified Messiah and Other Essays* (Minneapolis: Augsburg, 1974) 10–36.

pointedly, lets them invite him, and together with them celebrates messianic feasts (cf. Mark 2:15ff. with 1 Enoch 62:14). No
wonder that the Jews who are most sensitive in matters of
religious practice were enraged about this behavior and said
about Jesus: "Behold, a glutton and a drunkard, a friend of tax
collectors and sinners" (Matt 11:19; cf. also Luke 15:2).

Third scene: For pious Israelites nothing was—and continues to be—more sacred than the law that God had revealed
to his chosen people through Moses at Sinai. Jesus likewise was
raised in the fear of the law. Nevertheless, unlike any rabbi
before him, he instructed his disciples and the people in the
Sermon on the Mount: "You have heard that it was said [by
God] to the people of old, 'You shall not kill; and whoever kills
shall be liable to judgment'" (Matt 5:21–22). Or: "Again you
have heard that it was said to the people of old, 'You shall not
swear falsely, but shall perform to the Lord what you have
sworn.' But I say to you: Do not swear at all" (Matt 5:33–34; cf.
Jas 5:12). Here Jesus juxtaposes his own teaching with the revelation of God to the generation of the ancestors at Sinai, and
one cannot miss the critical sound of the contrast. In the case
of divorce Jesus even says that Moses allowed it to the Israelites
only for the sake of their hardness of heart, and then adds: "But
from the beginning [of creation] it was not so!" (Matt 19:8).
Even when Jesus affirms explicitly: "Do not think that I have
come to abolish the law and the prophets; I have come not to
abolish them but to fulfill them!" (Matt 5:17), one can hardly
blame his contemporaries for the impression that Jesus was
opposed to God's holy law.

Fourth scene: Instead of proffering the pious rich man a
way to take the "path of righteousness" that leads to eternal life
in the midst of his possessions, Jesus tells him to relinquish all
his possessions if he wants to be Jesus' disciple (Mark 10:17–22
par.). By means of the "pronouncement of woes" (from Luke
6:24–25) he further offends the numerous landed proprietors
and wealthy families of that period in Palestine and explains to
his disciples: "It is easier for a camel to go through the eye of a
needle than for a rich person to enter the kingdom of God"
(Mark 10:25).

Fifth incident: Among the insurrectionist and freedom party of the Zealots the imperial tolltax, introduced in AD 7, caused a revolt because they viewed it as the embodiment of the subjugation of God's people by godless pagans. The imperial denarius used to pay the tax, with its inscriptions and pictures lauding Caesar as God, they regarded as a symbol of idolatry. It was altogether impossible for any of them to accept Jesus' explanation: "Render to Caesar the things that are Caesar's and to God the things that are God's" (Mark 12:17). For them such a declaration was a flat betrayal of what was holy in Israel.

Finally the sixth scene: When Jesus moves to Jerusalem at the end of his ministry he decides on a provocative symbolic action. At one of the important ascents to the temple or—even more likely—in the so-called hall of pillars, he forbids the money changers their business, overturns the stands of those selling doves, and obstructs individuals who with their heavy loads want to move from the lower to the upper part of the city by using the temple bridges as a shortcut, thus traversing the temple area because of laziness.[8] Jesus substantiates his action

---

[8] On the meaning of Mark 11:16, see Christian Maurer, *TDNT*, 7:362; and Josephus, *Ag. Ap.* 2.106. Ernst Lohmeyer, *Das Evangelium nach Markus*, 11th ed. (MeyerK; Göttingen: Vandenhoeck & Ruprecht, 1951) 237 doubts the historicity of the Markan presentation in Mark 11:15–17 altogether. For him the story "can hardly be called an historical account, but rather a parenetic example with appended instruction. Historically one can barely recognize the incident as a whole, for it is difficult to imagine how Jesus is supposed to have cleansed the extensive court of the temple on his own, hence that the temple police did not intervene . . . or at least the Roman guard on the Antonia, so that this act was no issue in the case against Jesus." In *Was Jesus a Revolutionist?* (trans. William Klassen; Philadelphia: Fortress, 1971) 15–17, Martin Hengel traced the historical possibilities more carefully. He too considers a cleansing of the temple precinct by Jesus alone and without intervention by the Romans (as in Paul's case in Acts 21:27ff.) to be impossible: "According to Josephus, at the great feasts there were additional soldiers stationed on the roofs of the outer porches, who had the task of observing activities in the large outer court. [Note: Cf. *Ant.* 20.106–7; *J. W.* 2.224–25]. Any considerable tumult would inevitably have led to intervention by the garrison, especially since Pilate was not squeamish on this point. [Note: Cf. *Ant.* 18.55–62, 85–87.]" According to Hengel the Markan account is exaggerated because of narratival motivation, and Matthew and Luke have further intensified it. He concludes: "In the so-called temple cleansing we have, apparently, a prophetic demonstration or, one could also say, provocation, in which it was not a matter of driving out all those who sold and the money-

by saying: "Is it not written, 'My house shall be called a house
of prayer for all the nations'? But you have made it a den of
robbers" (Mark 11:17; cf. Isa 56:7 and Jer 7:11). For the priests
attending to the temple (cult) this is an incredible provocation.
No sacrifice can be paid for and no donation made to the temple
without the money changers, who convert the pilgrims' money
into the (Tyrian) temple currency. Forbidding the sale of doves
and small animals to the sellers of sacrificial animals means
questioning the nature of sacrifices as a whole. By means of his
temple cleansing Jesus endangers the entire order of the temple
cult, which God had established in the Torah. Henceforth the
powerful priesthood and the Sadducean nobility of Jerusalem,
heavily involved financially in the temple, join Jesus' mortal
enemies.

---

changers. We are dealing, rather, with a demonstrative condemnation of their
trade, a condemnation which was directed at the same time against the ruling
temple aristocracy, which derived profit from it. It may also be assumed here
that the word, not the action, stood at the center —such an isolated action
would have been meaningless by itself." If one considers Billerbeck's indications
(in Str-B 1:850–51) that the sale of sacrificial animals was practiced from the
Mount of Olives all the way to the temple mount, and further if one keeps in
mind the temple ascents that Benjamin Mazar has uncovered on the southern
side and on the southwestern corner of the temple area, one can reconstruct the
events more easily. Mazar points out that shops were already extant in the arches
of the pillars of the so-called Robinson's Arch (or ascent to the temple), "in
which goods were tendered for the needs of the visitors of the temple." He adds:
"It cannot be dismissed either that the hall of pillars [built in the shape of a
basilica, with a middle nave and two side naves] was used for trade associated
with the temple ritual. Here it was also possible to exchange foreign currency,
especially Roman, for coins used in Jerusalem." "Neue archäologische Ent-
deckungen in Jerusalem," David Flusser, ed., *Die letzten Tage Jesu in Jerusalem*
(trans. H. Zechner; Stuttgart: Calwer, 1982) 143–54; citations from 146, 147.
Since the hall of pillars, according to Mazar, "represented a separate entity on
its own right" (146), Jesus' prophetic-messianic symbolic action may have taken
place at one of the ascents to the temple (crowded with traders) or in the hall
of pillars itself. In view of the respect Jesus enjoyed, it seemed inopportune to
the (Jewish) authorities to proceed against Jesus at once. Only later (on the
following day, according to Mark 11:27ff.) did they call him to account. As Petr
Pokorný assumes in *The Genesis of Christology,* 48: "It was perhaps on this or
on a similar occasion that he uttered a *vaticinium* about the destruction of the
temple by way of a prophetic threat, which the evangelist later modified *ex
eventu* (Mark 13:2). This was clearly also the immediate occasion of the accusation against Jesus before the Sanhedrin."

In view of this sort of behavior on Jesus' part, if one reads in Deuteronomy 13 (and 17:1–7; 18:20) that a religious deceiver and false prophet must be eradicated from the people, the motive for the Jewish condemnation of Jesus by the high priests and Sadducees arises naturally: Jesus had to die because his public appearance, his teaching, and his (messianic) claim to authority violated the governing religious tradition of his people unbearably.

JESUS' MESSIANIC MISSION

If one inquires about the reason for Jesus' action, one encounters Jesus' messianic mission in all the incidents cited. For Jesus the baptism by John the Baptist meant the call to the public ministry as (messianic) Son of God (Mark 1:9–11 par.). Following his baptism Jesus set out to proclaim the message of the imminent kingdom of God (according to Isa 61:1–3) and, together with his disciples, to gather the eschatological people of God out of Israel (Luke 4:16ff.; Mark 3:13ff. par.). Through the provocative healings on the Sabbath Jesus asserts the kingdom of God against the powers of darkness opposing this kingdom. Jesus is "Lord of the Sabbath" (Mark 2:28) because, as the messianic Son of man, he ushers in the new, salutary order of creation.

In the instances of table fellowship with tax collectors and sinners, so offensive to the Pharisees, he wants to demonstrate to these humans whom the pious shun that God has mercy upon the sinner rather than upon the righteous (cf. Mark 2:17). To those who can least expect it he wants to give a foretaste of what it will mean to recline at table together with him, the Son of man, and with the patriarchs, Abraham, Isaac, and Jacob (cf. Matt 8:11).[9] Healings and table fellowship are practical symbols

---

[9] Otfried Hofius, *Jesu Tischgemeinschaft mit den Sündern* (Calwer Hefte 86; Stuttgart: Calwer, 1967) 20, formulates admirably: "Jesus' table fellowship with sinners is the bestowal and appropriation of God's forgiveness and the promise and giving of the kingdom of God in anticipation." One can recognize what is new and provocative in Jesus' actions if one compares the table fellow-

of God's reconciliation with humans through the mediatorship of Jesus.

The teaching of Jesus, whereby he does not want to abolish the law of Moses but instead transcend and fulfill it messianically, first of all summons his disciples, and then through them all Israel, to prepare anew for the loving will of a gracious God.

The critique of wealth and the call to renounce property arises from the understanding of Jesus, himself destitute (cf. Luke 9:58 par.), that it is not possible to serve God and unrighteous mammon at the same time (Luke 12:13 par.).

In his own way he can be unconcerned about the issue of the imperial tax because for him God's coming kingdom transcends the Zealots' political interests.

By means of the messianic, symbolic action of the cleansing of the temple Jesus questions the temple's priesthood (and Israel with them) about whether they intend to continue to carry out the atonement ritual without acquiescing to Jesus' message of repentance. Jesus sees that the time has come to worship God in the Spirit of truth and to cleanse the temple for such worship.

Despite all the criticism against him and the well-intentioned warnings not to carry things too far (cf. Mark 8:31–33; Luke 13:31–33), Jesus cannot desist from his controversial actions because that would mean denying his messianic mission. Accordingly the conflict between him and the main representatives of Israel's old religious order is unavoidable.

Jesus sees this conflict coming and does not avoid it. Already in Galilee he had taught his adherents that the love commandment did not apply only to neighbors and friends but also to the enemies and persecutors of Jesus' band: "You have heard that it was said [by God], 'You shall love your neighbor and hate your enemy.' But I say to you, Love your enemies and pray for those who persecute you, so that you may be children [υἱοί] of your Father who is in heaven" (Matt 5:43–44). When he sets out

---

ship of Jesus, the Son of man, which he had with tax collectors and sinners, to the early Jewish expectation found in 1 Enoch 62:14, namely that the "righteous" (who have been approved and tested in the final judgment) will one day be allowed to enjoy table fellowship with the Son of man. The price Jesus ultimately had to pay for his action was his life.

on his journey to Jerusalem some time later, he does not hide from his disciples that rejection, suffering, and death await him there. When Peter wants to dissuade him from this course, he levels a razor-sharp rebuke at him: "Get behind me, Satan! For you are not on the side of God, but of humans" (Mark 8:33). Jesus is clearly convinced that his path into suffering and death is God's inevitable intent (cf. Luke 13:33).

JESUS' COMPREHENSION OF HIS DEATH

Many exegetes and dogmatic theologians today are of the opinion that it was only the post-Easter community that attributed to Jesus the sayings in which he speaks about his suffering and sacrificial death. But together with Otto Betz,[10] Martin Hengel,[11] and others,[12] I think that the opposite is true. The post-Easter community learned the fact and the manner in which they were to understand Jesus' way of suffering to the cross directly from Jesus. One cannot infer the interpretation of Jesus' death as the vicarious death of the "Christ" (1 Cor 15:3) from the Easter events alone.

Jesus' willingness to take the path leading to death is quite historically plausible if, together with him, one is prepared to read the OT and concentrate especially on the book of Isaiah, which Jesus cites time and again.[13] Through the mouth of the

---

[10] Otto Betz, *Wie verstehen wir das Neue Testament* (Wuppertal: Aussaat, 1981) 34ff.

[11] Martin Hengel, *The Atonement* (trans. John Bowden; Philadelphia: Fortress, 1981). The English book is an expanded version of the essay: "Der stellvertretende Sühnetod Jesu. Ein Beitrag zur Entstehung des urchristlichen Kerygmas," *Internationale Katholische Zeitschrift* 9 (1980) 1–25; 135–47.

[12] To be cited first of all are Joachim Jeremias, *New Testament Theology* (trans. John Bowden; New York: Scribner's, 1971) 276–99; idem, *Jesus und seine Botschaft* (Stuttgart: Calwer, 1976) 61–77, 88–92; Leonhard Goppelt, *Theology of the New Testament* (trans. John Alsup; Grand Rapids: Eerdmans, 1981) 1:223–38; and Hans Walter Wolff, *Jesaja 53 im Urchristentum*, 4th ed. (Giessen: Brunnen, 1984) 55–71.

[13] For further consultation see Werner Grimm, *Die Verkündigung Jesu und Deuterojesaja* (2d ed.; Bern: Peter Lang, 1981) 231ff. In his study, *The Mystery of the Kingdom of God: The Secret of Jesus' Messiahship and Passion*

prophet God announces to his people in Isaiah 43:3–5 that he himself, out of love, will give people as a ransom for Israel. In fact, the oldest extant manuscript of Isaiah, the Qumran scroll of Isaiah (1QIsaᵃ), says: "because I love you I will give *the* human on your behalf [as a ransom]."[14] Isaiah 53 deals with the suffering servant of God. God's servant is sent and commissioned by God to bear vicariously the punishment for the sin of the people and thereby to procure Israel's salvation. Jesus' voluntary path into suffering and death makes good sense if he understood himself to be called to take the way of the suffering servant of God.

Jesus' famous declaration: "The Son of man did not come to be served but to serve and to give his life as a ransom for many" (Mark 10:45 par.), shows that he applies Isaiah 43:3–5 to his own pilgrimage. Instead of ruling and being served (cf. Dan 7:14), he himself is ready to serve "the many" to the point of death—as God determined it for his servant.[15] During the Last Supper in Jerusalem he gives the Twelve a share in the atoning power of his own "blood of the covenant" (Mark 14:24; cf. Exod 24:8), shed for "the many," according to Isaiah 53:11–12. One cannot wrest from the earthly Jesus this so-called saying of the cup, the one about the ransom in Mark 10:45, or the mysterious statement still shining through dimly in Mark 9:31: "The Son of man will be delivered [by God] into the hands of humans." These sayings of Jesus were lodged in the disciples' memory; from these saying they learned, after Easter, to grasp the mystery of the death of Jesus.[16]

(trans. Walter Lowrie; London: A. & C. Black, 1925) 236–39, which was as ingenious as it was imaginative, Albert Schweitzer already pointed out that the message of Second-Isaiah had a decisive influence upon Jesus' understanding of suffering (cf. the workbook edition supervised by R. Grabs: *Das Messianitäts—und Leidensgeheimnis: Eine Skizze des Lebens Jesu* vol. 5 [1974] 316–18).

[14] The article is surely to be understood generically (cf. GKC, §126*l*), though it can also be taken as a demonstrative, of course, in the context of Jesus' conception of being the (serving) Son of man himself.

[15] In the introduction to Wolff's monograph, *Jesaja 53*, I have endeavored to show how Jesus' messianic mission, the Son of man title, and the understanding of the passion are linked. On this matter see also ch. 1, "Jesus of Nazareth as the Christ of Faith."

[16] Cf. my essay, "Jesus von Nazareth und die neutestamentliche Christologie im Lichte der Heiligen Schrift," *Mitte der Schrift? Ein jüdisch-christliches*

In order to comprehend Jesus' willingness to suffer and to offer himself, expressed in these sayings, one needs to refer back once more to the OT-Jewish tradition of faith. In Luke 19:10 Jesus says concerning himself: "The Son of man came to seek and to save the lost [before God]." What does Jesus understand it to mean to be lost before God? For Jesus, as well as for the OT and for religious Judaism, sin is the actual and willful rebellion against God's will. Those who rebel against God's command-ment have to bear the deadly consequences of their action. The OT makes clear that humans who have renounced God can in no wise escape the death penalty. God will not be mocked and no injustice will abide in his holiness. Jesus is not only familiar with this perspective but also affirms it emphatically. At one point he says to his disciples: "For what does it profit a person, to gain the whole world and forfeit life? For what can a person give [to God] in return for life?" (Mark 8:36–37; cf. Ps 49:8–9). An individual who is lost before God (as well as a nation in sin) has only one chance for salvation, according to Jewish belief—by God having mercy upon the offenders out of unconstrained love and sparing them from having to bear themselves the deadly consequences of their sin. For the OT the cultic atonement represents the great opportunity, given by God, to free the people and the individual from their sins. The life of an animal, contained in the blood, is given up vicariously for that of the guilt-ridden individual(s) (Lev 17:11). But the life of the servant of God, too, can be a substitute for the ruined life of "the many," according to Isaiah 53:10ff.[17]

On this premise one can retrace Jesus' willingness to offer himself. During his ministry he realizes not only that the disci-ples he chose continue to be weak and susceptible to temptation (cf. Luke 22:31–32) but also that more and more people rebel against his message. At the same time he knows that this re-

---

Gespräch: Texte des Berner Symposions vom 6.-12. Januar 1985 (ed. Martin Klopfenstein, et al., Judaica et Christiana 11; Bern: Lang, 1987) 85–90.

[17] For an understanding of the atonement in the OT and NT, see Hartmut Gese, "The Atonement," *Essays on Bible Theology* (trans. Keith Crim; Minne-apolis: Augsburg, 1981) 93–116, and Bernd Janowski, *Sühne als Heilsgeschehen* (Neukirchen-Vluyn: Neukirchener, 1982).

sistance to his call to repentance and his person has deadly consequences for those concerned. Those who reject Jesus become guilty of the sin against the Holy Spirit (cf. Mark 3:28–29). In this threatening situation for his opponents, as well as for his disciples, Jesus decides to do the utmost he is capable of doing on earth: to offer himself to spare his friends and foes from the judgment of death. By means of his death Jesus does not appease a vengeful deity; rather, on his way of the cross he is the embodiment of the love of God, as sketched in Isaiah 43:3–4, 25. This love wants to spare the impenitent daughters and sons of Israel, as well as his feeble disciples, from having to perish because of their doubts about his mission and the consequences of their reserve toward Jesus' message. Even when he is nailed to the cross he does not curse his enemies but instead (like the servant of God) prays for them: "Father, forgive them, for they know not what they do" (Luke 23:34; cf. Isa 53:12). Jesus keeps the commandment to love the enemy even on the cross. To his friends and mortal enemies alike he wants to open up the possibility of one day realizing and confessing with the community of Isaiah 53: "Because the punishment [for our sins] was upon him, we are saved; by his wounds we are healed" (Isa 53:5).[18]

---

[18] Schweitzer, *Mystery of the Kingdom of God*, 240ff., assumes that Jesus adopted suffering unto death in order for the petition of the Lord's Prayer—and lead us not into temptation, but deliver us from evil—to be fulfilled. Temptation *(peirasmos)* refers to the premessianic tribulation, which was to take place prior to the coming of the kingdom, according to late Jewish eschatology. But Jesus did not instruct the believers about the atoning significance of his death, so that the disciples, who remained uncertain when he left, undertook a reinterpretation of Jesus' atoning death from the very inception of Christianity. Instead of speaking of Jesus' intent to suffer accordingly—that Jesus' atoning death was to relieve them of an atonement that they were to bring in this tribulation—they thought that through his death Jesus procured forgiveness of sins for them, and on that basis they would endure the judgment occurring when the kingdom of God breaks in. One should replace this fanciful assumption with Otto Betz's understanding, which the texts support much better: "Of particular importance is the statement in Mark 10:45: The Son of man sees the ultimate and highest purpose of his service in giving up his life for the many, that is to suffer death vicariously for a humanity subject to judgment. For since time was coming to a rapid close, the fact of unbelief and of refused repentance left no other choice to the one sent by God but to atone by his death for the sins of those whom he wanted to make the people of the *basileia*," *Wie verstehen wir das Neue Testament*, 34.

When one sees these correlations between the OT–Jewish tradition and Jesus' actions, Jesus' offering of himself becomes clear: He himself triggers the final mortal conflict in Jerusalem via the act of the temple cleansing.[19] For this reason he could not have been surprised that the priests of the temple and the nobles of the city take action against him. When the high priest has him apprehended in Gethsemane in the night of the Passover, he consciously refuses resistance. Before the members of the highest Jewish court who are hastily called together, he bluntly confesses his messianic mission, but then adds that one day his present judges would have to answer before him as the coming Son of man–judge of the world (Mark 14:61–62). Jesus indeed claims divine rights of sovereignty by means of this response to their question. On this premise the high priest and the Sanhedrin could regard Jesus as convicted of being a messianic deceiver of the people and a blasphemer of God who claimed God's laws for himself and who therefore had to be removed from the people.

Because they themselves have no authority to mete out the death sentence (John 19:31), they accuse Jesus before the Roman procurator of pretending to be a messiah, hence a politically dangerous insurrectionist. Pilate, the Roman, has little choice under these circumstances. In order to avoid a later rebellion, he has to act quickly. He has Jesus flogged and nailed to the cross as a deterrent. That this happens just outside Jerusalem on this major festival day is meant as a warning on the Romans' part. As far as the Jewish legal sensibilities are concerned, however, this is precisely in accordance with the special procedure governing the case of passing judgment against one who seduced the people. Following the Jewish law (t. *Sanh.* 11:7), such an individual is to be executed on one of the major pilgrim festivals, for the purpose of doing justice to the law,

---

[19] Jeremias, *New Testament Theology*, 1:279: "Above all, when Jesus decided to carry out the cleansing of the temple it must have been clear to him that he was risking his life; and that was in fact the occasion for the definitive official action against him." This understanding is supported not only by the historical reconstruction of the events of the passion, but also by the description of the temple cleansing in John 2:14–22.

which determines in Deuteronomy 17:13: "All the people are to hear, so that they might be afraid and will not be contemptuous again." Jesus has to die because his messianic ministry is unbearable to his opponents. Yet he takes his death upon himself knowingly and willfully, in order to atone for the sin of the many humans who reject him and for his feeble disciples.

Thus one confronts again Jesus' last words on the cross. According to the Gospel of Mark and of Matthew they are: "My God, my God, why have you forsaken me?" This sounds like a cry of despair. Indeed, the dying Jesus does lament his peril and dereliction to God. Yet he does not do it out of despair but as a final act of fearing God. Psalm 22 begins, "My God, my God, why have you forsaken me?" In this psalm the one who prays first laments his peril before God in order to be consoled with the salvation by the same God.[20] Jesus' lamenting cry, therefore, does not mean that in view of his death he despairs of his mission.[21] On the contrary! With his last words on earth Jesus entrusts himself prayerfully to his heavenly Father who, according to Jewish law and to Jesus' own confession, is the God who raises the dead (cf. Mark 12:27). Jesus' last cry: "My God, my God, *why . . .* ?" points beyond the cross to the divine *because.* God does indeed declare it on the third day after Jesus' death, according to the experience of the Easter witnesses. Hence in Romans Paul confesses together with the Christians before and alongside him: "For to this end Christ died and lived again, that he might be Lord both of the dead and of the living" (Rom 14:9).

---

[20] On understanding Ps 22, see esp. Hartmut Gese, "Psalm 22 und das Neue Testament: Der älteste Bericht vom Tode Jesu und die Entstehung des Herrenmahls," *Vom Sinai zum Zion: Alttestamentliche Beiträge zur biblischen Theologie* (Munich: Kaiser, 1974) 180–201.

[21] While Rudolf Bultmann, *Exegetica* (ed. Erich Dinkler; Tübingen: J. C. B. Mohr [Paul Siebeck], 1967) 452–53, considers the possibility that Jesus collapsed on account of the impending death, Wolfgang Schrage's interpretation of Jesus' final cry is more in line with the text. For him this word is "not merely an expression of abject despair or of pure senselessness because Jesus does not throw himself into the arms of despair but of God, though he did so *in* despair" "Das Verständnis des Todes Jesu Christi im Neuen Testament," *Das Kreuz Jesu Christi als Grund des Heils* (ed. Ernst Bizer, et al.; Gütersloh: Mohn, 1967) 67 n. 48.

The Problem of Interpretation

Thus one can give very diverse answers to the question, Why did Jesus have to die? They vary in intelligibility and yet they are all true historically.

There can be no doubt about the first answer: Jesus had to die because he made too many enemies who opposed his messianic ministry.

The second answer is more difficult: Jesus did not circumvent death because he viewed himself as called to take the way of the serving Son of man and of the suffering servant of God, whose death brings help and salvation to "the many" who are far from God. This answer is difficult because it begins to become intelligible only against the backdrop of the OT and because one has to continue to understand that Jesus' sacrifice was the sacrifice of love that the Father willed, so as to spare Jesus' friends and foes from perishing because of the consequences of their feebleness and rejection of Jesus.

The third answer is the most difficult because it includes a confession that, since the earliest days of Christianity, does not appeal to everyone: Jesus "died for our sins" and "was raised [by God] for our justification." He lived, suffered, and was raised in order to be and remain the one who reconciled God and humanity (cf. 1 Cor 15:3ff.; 2 Cor 5:21; Rom 3:25–26; 4:25; 8:3–4; etc.). Because in Romans 5:1–11 and 2 Corinthians 5:18–21 Paul speaks of the "reconciliation" through Christ and proclaims the "message of reconciliation" as gospel, he truly is "the messenger of Jesus" (A. Schlatter).[22]

---

[22] On the Pauline understanding of reconciliation, see Otfried Hofius, "Sühne und Versöhnung," *Versuche, das Leiden und Sterben Jesu zu verstehen* (ed. Wilhelm Maas; 1983) 25–46. Hofius also has the important reference to the fact that a satisfactory understanding of reconciliation has to do with a "theologically disastrous reversal of the Pauline statement of reconciliation" (44 n. 17). Precisely Jesus' own understanding of suffering and death nowhere points to a satisfaction demanded by God; rather one is to understand it as an act of representation. On behalf of God and in his nature as messianic Son of God, Jesus takes death upon himself, in order to keep his guilty friends and foes from the judgment of death.

For the theological interpretation this result has the following implication: The texts of the Gospels and Letters that speak of Jesus' vicarious and atoning death remain indispensable to all attempts at theological interpretation; they represent the standard whereby one can and must test whether the sayings concerning Jesus' death are in accordance with Scripture.

Nevertheless, one cannot ignore that the religious world of sacrifice is no longer a dynamic reality for people in the Western industrial nations. If it is essential to speak intelligibly about the meaning of Jesus' death with these people, it is necessary to choose a manner of expression that opens up the biblical texts without immediately presupposing a historical understanding of the biblical language of sacrifice. All the same, this manner of expression has to link today's people with the textual and experiential world of the Bible. One can find this manner of expression if one observes that Jesus himself, as well as the decisive texts in the apostolic letters, do not speak literally about the sacrifice and atonement through Jesus' vicarious death on the cross, but rather metaphorically.[23] The biblical texts speak of Jesus' sacrificial death and of the atonement effected by him; and they express that Jesus took the path of death *out of love* for his friends and foes, and that this love, ready to be offered up, is the love of *God*, who loves his people and his creatures even more fervently than a human mother, according to Isaiah 49:15.

We have explored the way the language and experience of love links the biblical texts with the modern experiential world. We too know and experience that love which, in its purest form,

---

[23] Jesus' sacrificial death is no cultic act that needs to be repeated, but the Son of God's vicarious yielding of life on Golgotha. In this manner and only for this reason is he able to discharge the cultic sacrifice of atonement once for all. The transference to which I refer is seen exegetically because Mark 10:45 par. and Mark 14:24 par. contain an interpretation of Jesus' mission and pro-existence *(Pro-Existenz)* that is itself based on Isa 43:3ff.; 53:12; and Exod 24:8. The text witnesses find their new and unique realization in Jesus' "existential representation" (H. Gese). One can make an analogous case for Rom 3:25, which, against the backdrop of Lev 16, contains a bold interpretation of the death on the cross that is critical of the cult. It is no different with Heb 9:24ff. On this issue, consult further Ferdinand Hahn, "Das Verständnis des Opfers im Neuen Testament," *Exegetische Beiträge zum ökumenischen Gespräch* (Göttingen: Vandenhoeck & Ruprecht, 1986) 1:262–302.

is self-sacrifice for others. Hence one can also answer the question of why Jesus had to die as follows: He had to die because his life's witness to God's unfathomable love for the poor and the lost breaks the religious standards of the powerful in Israel at that time. Jesus was ready to offer himself because he deemed the realization of God's love to be more important than his own life. One can understand Jesus' resurrection as confirmation of the victory of love over all human sin and over death. As messianic Son of man Jesus is the love of God personified (1 John 4:9–10, 16).

Even in this form of language the sayings about the meaning of Jesus' death remain difficult and demanding. Already in the biblical experience, and since then in a continually new Christian hermeneutical experience, these sayings are truly understood only when one engages in thought, word, and deed in the love of God. Indeed, understanding biblical texts is not merely a matter of the mind but also of the heart and of experience.

3

THE NEW TESTAMENT WITNESS
CONCERNING THE LORD'S SUPPER[1]

THE QUESTION CONCERNING THE TRADITION AS A WHOLE

THE MOST VALUABLE AND MOST IMPORTANT SALVIFIC TREASURE
entrusted to the church of Jesus Christ in this world is the gospel
of Jesus Christ. The gospel is the message of salvation, established by Jesus and proclaiming him as reconciler and Lord—a
message that needs to be declared, heard, and taken to heart. But

[1] In this chapter I combine three preliminary studies on the topic of the
Lord's Supper: "Vorüberlegungen unter neutestamentlichen Gesichtspunkten,"
on the issue of the Lord's Supper with children, in *Evangelium und Kirche*
(Rundbrief 3, 1979) 3–10; "Das Herrenmahl im Neuen Testament," *Das missionarische Wort: Zeitschrift für Verkündigung und Gemeindeaufbau* 36 (1983)
47–56; "Biblische Theologie als Weg der Erkenntnis Gottes," *JBT* 1 (1986)
91–114. I am grateful to my faculty colleagues, O. Bayer and M. Rössler, for their
willingness in the winter semester of 1983/84 to undertake an interdisciplinary
seminar on the topic "Lord's Supper and Lord's Supper Celebration." I dedicate
this essay to Martin Hengel as a token of my gratitude for twenty years of
mutuum colloquium and of *mutua consolatio fratrum*. I limit references to the
essential minimum, given the space limitations.

the gospel also needs to be learned and experienced. The celebration of the Lord's Supper is the most important and ecclesi-
astically the most meaningful occasion to this end.

Our celebrations of the Lord's Supper in worship services
or other church-related contexts today are ordered by all of the
given church tradition, and we thereby pursue a present-day
task of proclamation. Whereas the present-day Lord's Supper
celebrations vary from place to place and from time to time, the
church tradition represents a mature continuum, determining
our action, our thought, and our expectations from the Lord's
Supper celebration. In the Protestant realm the liturgical relation to the so-called accounts of institution are constitutive for
the Lord's Supper celebrations. But this relation remains em-
bedded in a liturgical frame that did not arise until the post-
biblical era and in an interpretive tradition that is centuries old,
highly diversified, and frequently directed by formulations of
questions that were biblically remote, yet inescapable in terms
of the history of the church and of ideas. For this reason they
also found their reflection in the liturgical tradition. For example, one may refer to the question of the manner of Christ's
presence in the celebration and in the Lord's Supper elements,
or to the discussion of who is to preside at the Lord's Supper
and which words and kinds of action have to determine the
celebration in order to vest it with ecclesiastical worth.

The following formulation of the question is directed to
the Lord's Supper tradition, as it has come down to us in the NT.
Although one can and must differentiate within the NT tradition
of the Lord's Supper, such differentiation must not distort the
view that the liturgy of the church and the exegetical account-
ability to the Holy Scriptures as a whole necessitate inquiry into
the entire tradition. We do not celebrate the Lord's Supper
alternatively in line with the earthly Jesus or Paul or the Gospel
of John, but as directed by the Scriptures bringing together as a
canon not only the OT and the NT, but also the four Gospels, the
letters of Paul, Acts, the Catholic Letters, Hebrews, and the
Apocalypse of John. Despite the necessary and even instructive
differentiation within the Lord's Supper tradition, one has to be
concerned with the complete biblical witness of the Lord's

Supper that arose historically. Only this totality became liturgically determinative and may continue to be understood as authoritative in a church that derives its self-understanding from the Scriptures. A glance at the monograph by Xavier Léon-Dufour, *Sharing the Eucharistic Bread*, teaches us that we do not pursue merely a Protestant goal by starting with all of Scripture. He observes, "The object of exegetical work is by definition not this or that text removed from its context in the Bible as a whole and declared to be more accurate than any other. The object is the total biblical datum that we call 'canonical.' Exegetes must think of themselves as 'biblical theologians' or they will not do justice to the revealed datum as it really is."[2]

AGREEMENTS AND DIVERGENCIES IN THE TRADITION

One has to proceed carefully with the interpretation of the biblical texts of the Lord's Supper. The four so-called accounts of institution presented in the Gospels and in Paul (Matt 26:26–29; Mark 14:22–25; Luke 22:14–20; and 1 Cor 11:23–26) are formulated tersely and each word in them is carefully chosen. Although the texts indicate considerable commonality, they are also shaped differently and placed in such diverse frameworks that one has to focus on agreements as well as divergencies in the tradition.

I address the most important divergencies first.

1. The Gospels according to Mark and Luke narrate the farewell supper of Jesus in the context of the story of Jesus' suffering and death; the same is also true (despite some editing) of the Gospel of Matthew. In Paul, however, one confronts a text that only briefly alludes to the events "in the night when the

---

[2] Xavier Léon-Dufour, *Sharing the Eucharistic Bread: The Witness of the New Testament* (trans. Matthew J. O'Connell; New York: Paulist, 1987) 5. Pointing in the same direction are Ferdinand Hahn's "Thesen zur Frage einheitsstiftender Elemente in Lehre und Praxis des urchristlichen Herrenmahls," *Kirche: Festschrift für Günther Bornkamm zum 75. Geburtstag* (ed. Dieter Lührmann and Georg Strecker; Tübingen: J. C. B. Mohr [Paul Siebeck], 1980) 415–24.

Lord was betrayed" (1 Cor 11:23–26) and then proceeds to recall the standard account for the Corinthian community's celebration of the Lord's Supper. Thus although the three Synoptic Gospels primarily narrate the Lord's Supper and the community's celebration of the Lord's Supper is viewed only from the perspective of these narratives, the opposite is the case in Paul. He offers a piece of ritual in narrative form and, in doing so, presupposes familiarity with the story of Jesus' passion.

2. But the differences are more extensive. The words whereby Jesus comforts his disciples directly at the farewell supper and that we generally label far too vaguely as "words of interpretation" or "words of institution" read differently in the four texts before us. Although Mark and Matthew on the one hand and Luke and Paul on the other are in close harmony in their formulations, both offer such divergent renditions that it is difficult to say whether Mark and Matthew or Paul and Luke have preserved the more original form of the so-called *verba testamenti*.

3. Whereas Jesus does not speak the following words until the end of the Lord's Supper in Mark (and Matthew): "Truly, I say to you, I shall not drink again of the fruit of the vine until that day when I drink it new in the kingdom of God" (Mark 14:25), Jesus declares his renunciation of food and drink already before the (Passover) meal begins, according to the Lukan narrative (cf. Luke 22:15–16). Above all, Mark and Matthew give the impression that Jesus ate the Passover meal with his disciples, interpreted the bread and wine during the meal, gave them to his disciples, and finally directed his focus to the heavenly table fellowship to come. According to Luke, however, Jesus foregoes all food and drink from the start, immediately focuses on the meal of fulfillment in the coming kingdom of God, and during the meal gives bread and wine only to those at table with him, to whom he spoke the "words of institution."

4. To top off the difficulties, the Gospel of John narrates Jesus' farewell meal very differently from the other three Gospels and from Paul. While Mark, Matthew, and Luke report that Jesus held the Passover with his disciples and in that context celebrated the Lord's Supper, and while Paul likewise speaks of the meal "in the night in which Jesus was betrayed," according

to the Johannine passion narrative Jesus is already laid to rest in the tomb in the evening of the Passover. Jesus' farewell meal with his own, described in John 13, is celebrated on the eve of the Passover, the focal point of the meal is the scene of the foot washing, and nothing is said about the institution of the Lord's Supper. In its place, in the framework of Jesus' Bread-of-Life discourse in John 6:52–58, the allusion to eating Jesus' flesh and drinking Jesus' blood is so strong that one has the impression that this is the Johannine interpretation of the Lord's Supper.

Hence the NT texts concerning the Lord's Supper pose a number of questions, not all of which can be resolved ultimately. Even the following reflections represent merely one attempt to shed light upon the intrabiblical history of the Lord's Supper and in this way move on to the tradition as a whole. There are other attempts alongside this one, and the divergent form of the texts compels one to remain open to different attempts at explanation. In this presentation I adhere to the following five principles.

1. From a literary perspective all the NT (Lord's Supper) texts originate from the post-Easter witness tradition; hence one must evaluate them exegetically primarily as witness texts. As the post-Easter accounts and rituals already mentioned suggest, one can use the texts to argue back to the history of the Lord's Supper.

2. In the history of tradition the description of the three Gospels according to Matthew, Mark, and Luke is supported historically by apostolic traditions that reach back into the pre-Easter period of Jesus' life and are generally reliable.[3] These traditions enable one to come closer to the earthly Jesus than does the Johannine tradition, whose main emphasis is the post-Easter understanding of Jesus effected by the Spirit.

3. The original context of Jesus' farewell meal with the Twelve was a Passover meal, therefore, as the Synoptics report

---

[3] On this view of the tradition, see my essay, "The Theme: The Gospel and the Gospels," *The Gospel and the Gospels* (ed. Peter Stuhlmacher; Grand Rapids: Eerdmans, 1991) 1–25, and the literature cited there; Rainer Riesner, *Jesus als Lehrer*, 2d ed. (Tübingen: J. C. B. Mohr [Paul Siebeck], 1984); and Birger Gerhardsson, "The Path of the Gospel Tradition," *The Gospel and the Gospels*, 75–96; idem., *The Gospel Tradition* (ConBNT 17; Lund: Gleerup, 1986).

synonymously. Only where absolutely required to do so should one depart from this account.[4]

4. The Gospel of John (clearly more distant from the first three Gospels) begins with a different chronology for the unfolding of Jesus' passion: As the true Passover lamb Jesus dies on the cross at the time of the slaying of the Passover lambs in the temple (cf. John 1:29, 36; 18:28; 19:36). Because of this portrayal the Fourth Gospel cannot furnish an account of the institution of the meal in the context of the Passover meal as recorded in the Synoptics. One finds the Johannine interpretation of the Lord's Supper in the Bread-of-Life discourse of John 6.

5. In the inquiry into the original wording of the "words of institution," one should give preference (as in the history of the text in general) to the version that most easily clarifies historically the origin of the other versions; this version is found in Mark, not in Luke or Paul.

At the conclusion I come back once more to these five principles and to the association with the Lord's Supper texts arising from them.

THE TABLE FELLOWSHIP BEFORE GOD

If one wants to understand Jesus' farewell meal in the intimate circle of his disciples, it is essential first to be aware that

---

[4] While Markus Barth, *Das Mahl des Herrn* (Neukirchen-Vluyn: Neukirchner, 1987) 36–37; abridged in *Rediscovering the Lord's Supper* (Atlanta: John Knox, 1988) 15ff., attributes major theological significance to the fact that the Synoptics describe Jesus' farewell meal as a Passover meal, Léon-Dufour, *Sharing*, 306–8, has most recently attempted to show, in discussion with Joachim Jeremias, *The Eucharistic Words of Jesus* (trans. Norman Perrin, rev. ed.; New York: Scribner's, 1966) 15–88, that Jesus' farewell meal could hardly have been a Passover meal. Regrettably he does not answer the counterquestion of why the Synoptics speak of Jesus' farewell Passover all the same. But as long as this decisive question in the history of tradition cannot be answered at all or only in terms of assumptions, it is imperative exegetically to begin with the synoptic version of the narrative. This avenue has correctly been taken, e.g., by Rudolf Pesch, *Das Abendmahl und Jesu Todesverständnis* (QD 80; Freiburg, Basel, Vienna: Herder, 1978).

for Jesus himself and his Jewish contemporaries the celebration of the meal is the embodiment of peaceful fellowship with God and with one another in the presence of God.

Isaiah 25:6–8 describes the meal as central event in the future kingdom of God:

> On this mountain [of Zion, in Jerusalem] the LORD of hosts will make for all peoples a feast of rich food, a feast of well-aged wines, of rich food filled with marrow, of well-aged wines strained clear. And he will destroy on this mountain the shroud that is cast over all peoples, the sheet that is spread over all nations; he will swallow up death forever. Then the Lord GOD will wipe away the tears from all faces, and the disgrace of his people he will take away from all the earth, for the LORD has spoken (NRSV).

According to a tradition contained in a Jewish apocalypse, not written until after but nevertheless older than Jesus' death, the so-called Ethiopic Enoch, those acknowledged as righteous in the last judgment may enjoy everlasting table fellowship in the presence of God, together with the Son of man–Messiah (1 Enoch 62:13–14). Even before the farewell meal in Jerusalem Jesus pointed to this meal in God's kingdom (cf. Matt 8:11–12 par. Luke 13:28–29).

Knowing this expectation sheds new light on the varied Gospel accounts of Jesus' table fellowship with the tax collectors and sinners (cf. Mark 2:15ff. par. Matt 9:10ff.; Luke 5:29ff.; 19:1ff.). According to Mark 2:17 par., Jesus knows he is sent to call sinners to repentance and to offer them God's forgiveness. This became a dynamic reality in the occasions of his table fellowship. At Jesus' side the participants in those meals are allowed to experience a foretaste of the heavenly table fellowship of the Son of man with the righteous. Although in Jewish expectation the heavenly Son of man will recline at table in God's presence only with the righteous he acknowledged in the judgment, those who were at table with Jesus are publicly known sinners and outlaws. According to Luke 15:2; Matthew 11:19 par. Luke 7:34, Jesus' reception of them appears to his critics to be provocative and unacceptable. Jesus, however, seems to have started from the premise that those at table with him, in his presence, are already sanctified and justified before God on account of his prayer and his willingness to offer himself (cf. Mark 10:45 par.). In any case, turning to Zacchaeus he says: "the Son of man came to seek and to save the lost" (Luke 19:10). The consequence of Jesus' commitment to his messianic mission in regard to this and other aspects is that it gradually earns him the enmity of all the major Jewish groups.

Jesus' Farewell Passover

The final break comes when Jesus journeys to Jerusalem on the occasion of the Passover (in AD 30 or 31) and is hailed as Messiah king when he enters there. He speaks of the destruction of the temple and the holy city of Jerusalem, and, to top it all, demonstratively expels the money changers and traders of sacrificial animals from the temple precinct. The high priest and the Jewish high court determine to end Jesus' activities and to have him executed. Judas offers them the opportunity to arrest the man from Nazareth at a distance from the festive throng[5] (cf. Mark 14:2 par.) and concealed by the night. Jesus does not elude this development. On the contrary, with full awareness he precipitates it with the so-called cleansing of the temple (Mark 11:15–17 par.) and with his provocative preaching during the final days in Jerusalem (cf., e.g., Mark 12:1–12 par. and 12:18–27 par.). He does not contemplate escaping. The only thing he still wants to do prior to his end is to celebrate the Passover with his disciples, in keeping with the ancient custom of the pilgrims: "I have earnestly desired to eat this Passover with you before I suffer" (Luke 22:15).

---

[5] On this understanding of Mark 14:2 par., see Jeremias, *Eucharistic,* 65–67. Günther Bornkamm, *Jesus of Nazareth* (trans. Irene and Fraser Mc-Luskey with James M. Robinson; London: Hodder and Stoughton, 1960) 159–62, insists, without providing any reasons, on the refuted (by Jeremias) sense of "before the festival" (159) and on this premise puts in question the entire issue of the synoptic chronology of the passion. In terms of the history of tradition and of theology, Bornkamm does not clarify either why the "conception of Jesus' Last Supper as the Passover meal goes back to the theology of the first three Evangelists, and to that of the Christian groups behind them" (*Jesus,* 162).

For Israelites the Passover is far more than a festive family meal. It has to do with commemorating Israel's deliverance from Egypt in the form of a ritual communal meal. At the time of Jesus the slaughtering of the Passover lambs was allowed only in the temple of Jerusalem (cf. Deut 16:5). For this reason thousands of Jews undertook the pilgrimage to Jerusalem every year, there to celebrate the Passover in its fullest sense. Those outside Jerusalem had to celebrate the Passover evening without a Passover lamb. (After the destruction of the temple in AD 70 this type of celebration necessarily became the common practice; only the Samaritans maintained the killing of the Passover lambs on Mt. Gerizim.) It was the custom of the pilgrims to group together in numbers large enough to consume a Passover lamb together. They were required to have the meal in Jerusalem and also to spend the Passover night in the city (cf. Deut 16:6–7). Jesus conforms to this custom. He instructs his disciples to prepare everything according to regulation (Mark 14:12ff. par.) and comes to Jerusalem in the evening to celebrate the meal in the circle of his closest friends. The twelve disciples with whom he keeps the last Passover are for him the representatives of the eschatological Israel, the nation of twelve tribes, whom he wants to gather by means of his message (cf. Matt 19:28 par. Luke 22:28–29). Because Jesus celebrates only with the Twelve as representatives of the new people of God, no women or children are present.

In keeping with the OT regulations concerning the Passover (Exod 12:1, 14; 13:3–10; Deut 16:1–8) and the ancient Jewish festival order, the evening celebration is to remember Israel's exodus from Egypt, the ratification of the covenant at Sinai according to Exodus 24, the giving of the Torah, the leading into the promised land, and the building of the temple to atone for sins. Together everyone sings Psalms 113–118 in praise of God, the so-called Hallel, and is mutually encouraged in the hope of the ultimate redemption of Israel from all affliction and trouble. This has remained the case to this day, and the following has applied ever since the Mishnah tractate concerning the Passover (Pesaḥ. 10:5): "In every generation the individual is obligated to view himself as though he himself had left Egypt, for it says: On

account of what the Lord did to *me* when *I* moved out of Egypt"
(Exod 13:8).

With regard to Jesus' conduct during the farewell Passover,
the oldest NT texts relative to the Lord's Supper (in parallel to
the Mishnah) capture only Jesus' conspicuous actions and expressions that go beyond the common festival customs. How the
Passover was celebrated, what was eaten when, and which cup
was taken up and drunk, did not seem to be worth mentioning
to those who passed on the earliest Jewish Christian tradition,
because everyone was still familiar with the origin of the tradition. (Only in the Gentile Christian realm and in the course of
continuing the tradition the ancient accounts did the Jewish
Passover sink into oblivion and hence become a matter of
contention in the interpretation of the texts.)[6] If one follows the
common witness of the first three Gospels and if one inserts
Jesus' actions into the ritual sequence of the Passover meal,[7] one
sees Jesus with his disciples in Jerusalem observing the festival
of Israel's deliverance from slavery in Egypt (cf. Mark 14:17–26
par.). Yet in the midst of the festival he already celebrates far
more than merely the redemption of the past!

As the skilled Jewish Christian reader is able to derive from
Mark 14:17–25, and especially from Luke 22:14–20, Jesus fo-

---

[6] This equally important perspective in the history of tradition and
methodology is all too easily ignored in the discussion of the Lord's Supper
texts. One should carefully distinguish the mostly "Gentile Christian" horizon
of reception of modern exegetes from that of the first Jewish Christian tradents
and recipients.

[7] Cf. the overview in Jeremias, *Eucharistic*, 79–80, or also Pesch, "Abendmahl," 76–77. The Passover meal has four main parts:

A. Preliminary course: Head of household blesses the first cup (kiddush
cup). Eating vegetables, bitter herbs, compound formed of nuts, fruits, and wine
(haroseth). The meal is dished up (but not yet served), the second cup is mixed
and filled (but not yet drunk).

B. Passover liturgy: Head of household recites the Passover haggadah
(Aramaic). Part one of the Passover Hallel (Hebrew) = Pss 113, 114. Drinking
of the second cup (haggadah cup).

C. Festival meal: Grace spoken by the head of household over the
unleavened bread. Meal (Passover lamb, matzoth, bitter herbs, *haroseth*, wine).
Grace over the third cup (cup of blessing).

D. Conclusion: Pouring the fourth cup. Part two of the Passover Hallel
(Hebrew) = Pss 115–118. Praise over the fourth cup (Hallel cup).

cused his peculiar sayings and actions in the farewell Passover
on the main course itself. He carried out the customary ritual
of the preliminary course and of the Passover liturgy. For the
main course, however, the Passover haggadah no longer contained definitive liturgical rules. This is where Jesus begins: with
the custom of the prayer at the beginning and end of the meal.
The unleavened bread and the bitter herbs had previously been
interpreted in the Passover liturgy; Jesus newly interprets the
occasion of the host saying the prayer of thanksgiving for the
bread (unleavened, of course, in the Passover night), of breaking
the bread, and dividing it among those at table by speaking the
words that we now call "the bread saying." This saying is followed by the Passover meal itself. At the conclusion of this meal
and before everyone drank the cup, it was customary for the
head of the table, the host, to speak the prayer of thanksgiving
over the third cup, the "cup of blessing" (1 Cor 10:15)—or, as
Luke and Paul elucidate correctly (1 Cor 11:25; Luke 22:20), the
cup "after the meal." This custom provides Jesus with the opportunity to speak "the cup saying" and, particularly notewor-
thy, to allow all those at table with him to drink from one single
cup of blessing.

As the eschatological perspective in Mark 14:25 par. shows
and as Luke 22:15–16 impresses further, Jesus places all the
actions associated with the meal in an eschatological light. In
his mind's eye he already anticipates the messianic table fellowship in the presence of God and wants to include his disciples
symbolically in this eschatological table fellowship. The pros-
pect of the messianic meal in Mark 14:25 par. or Luke 22:15–16
is not a superfluous development or a pronouncement merely
anticipating the Lord's Supper text, but is the decisive indica-
tion of the goal that Jesus has in focus. In Jerusalem Jesus
celebrates with the Twelve, on the borderline between his impending death and the new life in the messianic fulfillment. In
this connection he openly expresses that which procures the
disciples' access to the eschatological table fellowship. For them
his own vicarious death opens up "access to God" (Rom 5:2),
sets them at peace with their heavenly Father, and allows them
to share in the messianic meal of Isaiah 25:6–8 and in the new

covenant promised in Jeremiah 31:31ff., taking the place of the covenant at Sinai and completing it (cf. Jer 31:32–33).

THE WORDS OF ADMINISTRATION

Jesus does not compare or identify himself with the Passover lamb in any of the Lord's Supper texts transmitted in the NT. This identification occurs only in retrospection upon Jesus' accomplished passion and resurrection in 1 Corinthians 5:7; 1 Peter 1:19; John 1:29, 36, and probably also Revelation 4:6; 5:12, and 13:8. At the beginning of the main course of the Passover meal, after the prayer of thanksgiving for the bread, Jesus himself tells his disciples that what they are now eating together is not only the "bread of affliction" (cf. Deut 16:3) of the Passover, as it was known in the liturgy. Rather, by eating the bread they are obtaining a share in him who is about to face death for them.

The simplest and oldest form preserved (by Mark) records the first words of Jesus as addressing his disciples openly: "Take, this is my body." The Lukan and Pauline tradition clarifies this saying of Jesus further: "This is my body which is for you" (1 Cor 11:24), or "This is my body which is given for you" (Luke 22:19). Within the Jewish scope of the Passover meal celebration this word means far more than merely Jesus' identification with the bread. The original, Aramaic form of Jesus' words of administration did not use the Greek auxiliary verb "is"; for this reason the original meaning of the words of administration cannot be derived definitively from the "is," no matter how important it may have become in the history of interpretation. That with which Jesus is concerned is a life-giving process as a whole: By jointly hearing Jesus' prayer of thanksgiving and encouragement, and eating the bread that Jesus broke and gave to them, they obtain a share in the substitutionary existence of Jesus, who offers himself vicariously on their behalf. By sharing in Jesus' relinquishing of his life the disciples are prepared for the eschatological meal. He himself is the bread that Jesus gives them, he is the one who grants them new life in peace with God and with each other through his sacrificial death. Jesus' prayer of thanksgiving, the breaking of bread, the word concerning the bread, the distribution to the disciples, and their eating it with one another, all this belongs together and represents a messianic symbolic action.[8] This symbolic action is concerned with the bequest of fellowship between Jesus and those at table with him in the presence of God (cf. 1 Cor 10:16–17).

Historically the Passover meal followed this (initial) event of Jesus' self-impartation. It may well have been filled with table talk about what Jesus had meant with his words of administration and what hope and obligation for the disciples would arise from Jesus' readiness to offer himself. The Gospel of Luke intends to convey an impression of this table conversation in Luke 22:21–38. Likewise John's Gospel, in chapters 13–16, contains a number of discourses to be understood as farewell discourses in the context of the last meal.

The Jewish regulations for the Passover celebration make provision for only a brief word of praise to be spoken over the

---

[8] Christian Wolff, *Der erste Brief des Paulus an die Korinther*, part 2 (THKNT 7/2; Berlin: Evangelische Verlagsanstalt, 1982) 89–90, correctly seeks to understand the words of institution against the backdrop of the prophetic symbolic actions recounted in the OT; he refers to their fine explanation by Gerhard von Rad, *The Message of the Prophets* (trans. D.M.G. Stalker; London: SCM, 1965) 74–75, but points out at the same time that Jesus' parabolic action in the Last Supper expresses "his eschatological claim of authority," rather than merely a prophetic one. Heinz Schürmann, "Das Weiterleben der Sache Jesu im nachösterlichen Herrenmahl," *Jesu ureigener Tod* (Freiburg and Vienna: Herder, 1975) 90ff., aptly designates Jesus' actions in the Lord's Supper as "eschatological fulfillment signs." As far as the understanding of the *verba testamenti* is concerned, Markus Barth, *Das Mahl des Herrn*, 26, formulates with provocative clarity: "What has been said, e.g., concerning the unleavened bread and the cup of wine in the context of the Jewish Passover festival . . . could not possibly be intended and understood as miracle-working words of power, as magic formuli or as precise scientific descriptions of substances or alterations of substance. It was not the essence or the accidence of the blood and meat of lambs, or of unleavened bread and genuine wine that were up for discussion and called for explanation. The notion of transubstantiation or consubstantiation was as remote as was the expectation that a secret metaphysical function be grasped. Instead it is the so-called words of signification that need to be considered as the (abridged) table speeches responding to a very specific question." As in the Jewish Passover meal, this question is: Why are we celebrating in this manner? What is the purpose of this custom?

cup of blessing (the third cup) after the meal. But Jesus raises the cup, speaks the prayer of thanksgiving, and once more adds a special word of affirmation to his disciples: "This is my blood of the covenant, which is poured out for many" (Mark 14:24). Again Mark's version of the word of the cup is the most original and materially the most difficult one. It explains the other versions more easily than vice versa. What Jesus means thereby becomes clear only if one bears carefully in mind the biblical scope of language and expectation surrounding this statement. One again observes exegetically that the introductory "This [is]. . ." in Mark and Matthew refers to the cup and that the auxiliary verb "is" was not added until the Greek translation of the cup saying. Likewise in the case of the cup saying one should not only observe the identification of the content of the cup and Jesus' blood, but also inquire into the relationship of the event as a whole that this saying expresses. Jesus' prayer of thanksgiving over the cup, the saying concerning the cup, and their drinking together from the one cup belong together (cf. 1 Cor 10:16) and, as in the case of the bread saying, are to be appreciated as messianic symbolic action.

What is intended thereby is indicated in the individual formulations. Already the one cup that Jesus passed around is highly significant symbolically. According to rabbinic expectation all Israel will be given to drink from one enormous "cup of blessing" (cf. Ps 116:13) at the meal of the nations on Zion. In anticipation of this act of God's redeemed people drinking together from one cup, Jesus allows the Twelve to drink from the one cup as representatives of the new people of God.[9] In this manner they all obtain a share in the atoning effect of the blood shed for them. Thus in the cup saying, too, Jesus gives the utmost of what he is able to give—his life that he offers up for

---

[9] Schürmann, "Weiterleben," 76, correctly sees a decisive difference over against the Jewish (meal) tradition in that "in the Christian celebration, corresponding with the distribution of the bread to all, *the one cup* of the head of the household is also handed to all those at the table." After David Daube pointed out to me the Jewish expectation indicated in the text above at a Passover celebration in Jerusalem (April 1984), it seems to me to be likely that the giving of the one cup already represents a symbolic act of Jesus. On the early Jewish expectation mentioned above, cf. Str-B IV/1: 72; IV/2: 628, 1146–47, 1163–64.

"the many." Life (human or animal) is in the blood, as far as the OT and Judaism are concerned. Blood belongs to God alone and is to be used only in the ritual of the atoning sacrifice in the temple. Leviticus 17:11–12 states: "For the life of the flesh is in the blood; and I have given it for you upon the altar to make atonement for your souls; for it is the blood that makes atonement, by reason of the life." Based on this perspective Jesus' blood refers to Jesus' life that he is to offer for "the many," in order to atone for them. In the OT the expression "to shed blood" means—as it does in today's language—"to take someone's life by force" (cf., e.g., Gen 9:6; Num 35:33; Deut 21:7).

In the cup saying, when Jesus speaks of his blood shed for the many, he has in mind his impending violent death and the substitutionary yielding up of his life "for the many" contained in it. The expression "the many," which seems strange today, refers to the countless masses and alludes to Isaiah 53:11: "by his suffering my servant shall make *many* righteous by taking their iniquities upon himself." In the Lord's Supper Jesus understands himself to take the part of the suffering servant of God who brings about righteousness and peace for Israel through his life and death. As servant of God and Son of man who suffers vicariously, Jesus reconciles God with the Twelve and grants them a new being in righteousness (cf. Isa 53:11–12 and Mark 10:45 par.). The word that speaks of the "blood of the covenant" in the context of the Passover meal reminds one of Exodus 24:8, where Moses sprinkles the people with the "blood of the covenant" in order to execute and ratify the Sinai covenant between God and Israel. The ancient Targum on this passage addresses the atoning effect of the "blood of the covenant" in Exodus 24, hence there would not have to be any dispute about the theological meaning of the blood (of Jesus) with reference to its atonement.[10]

---

[10] The unending attempts to keep the aspect of the atoning sacrifice away from the Lord's Supper sayings, to speak at best of a representative offering up of Jesus' life on the cross, and to trace back the atonement-theology interpretation of Jesus' death to no earlier than the early Christian community (cf., e.g., Ferdinand Hahn, "Das Verständnis des Opfers im Neuen Testament," *Exegetische Beiträge zum ökumenischen Gespräch* [Göttingen: Vandenhoeck & Ru-

(Zechariah 9:11 recalls the "blood of the covenant" as well. In part the Jewish interpretation has understood the blood of the covenant in Zechariah 9:11 to refer not only to the blood of the covenant according to Exodus 24:8, but also to the blood shed at the time of the male Israelites' entrance into the Abrahamic covenant—in circumcision.[11] To Jewish ears, therefore, the expression "blood of the covenant" may carry an additional meaning. In this case the issue is the blood that guarantees God's covenant with his people, beginning with Abraham, via the covenant made at Sinai, for all eternity. Nevertheless, this interpretation of Zechariah 9:11 has not gained a broad follow-

---

precht, 1986] 1:277ff., 283ff.), have their theological-historical roots in Protestantism (cf. Ulrich Wilckens, *Der Brief an die Römer* [EKKNT 6/1; Zurich: Benziger; Neukirchen-Vluyn: Neukirchener, 1978] 233–43). All of them appear contrived and historically forced against the tradition of the text. The (only, in my opinion) correct venue of interpretation is indicated by Martin Hengel (following Jeremias, *Eucharistic*) and Pesch, "Abendmahl": "On the night before his death, 'in which he was betrayed' (or 'delivered up': I Cor 11.23), Jesus celebrated the passover meal with his disciples and in it—presumably in parallel to the traditional words of interpretation which explained what was happening at the meal—in a symbolic action he related the broken bread to the breaking of his body and at the end of the meal the wine in the cup of blessing to the pouring out of his blood, through which the new eschatological covenant with God would be founded and atonement would be achieved for all. In this way, at the same time he represented his imminent death as the eschatological saving event which—in connection with Isa. 53—in the context of the dawn of the kingdom of God brought about reconciliation with God for all Israel, indeed for all humans, and sealed God's eschatological new covenant with his creatures. . . . Their encounter with the risen Lord confirmed for the disciples this legacy of Jesus, the meaning of which had been overshadowed by the catastrophe of the sudden arrest and shameful crucifixion of Jesus and their own failure, which immediately followed. It was not primarily their own theological reflections, but above all the interpretative sayings of Jesus at the Last Supper which showed them how to understand his death properly. As a saying of Jesus, Mark 10.45 probably also belongs in the context of that last night; it will have been used by him to elucidate his mysterious symbolic action. . . . The saying over the cup and the saying about ransom are connected by the universal service 'for the many', in the sense of 'for all', which is presumably to be derived from Isaiah 53. This boundlessness of the appropriation of salvation matches the freedom of the proclamation and the activity of Jesus towards all the outcast, the lost and the sinners in Israel"; Martin Hengel, *The Atonement* (trans. John Bowden; Philadelphia: Fortress, 1981) 72–73.

[11] See Jeremias, *Eucharistic*, 217 n. 5; and Str-B, vol. 4, pt. 1, p. 39.

ing. Hence Exodus 24:8 remains the governing text to which one must adhere.)

Exodus 24:9–11 narrates that Moses, together with Aaron and seventy elders of Israel, ascended the mount of God after the sprinkling with the blood of the covenant. There they all were allowed to behold God and had a meal in his presence without perishing (as sinners) on account of God's glory: God "did not raise his hand against the leaders of the Israelites; they beheld God and they ate and drank" (Exod 24:11). In the cup saying Jesus evidently has this scene in mind but at the same time focuses upon the eschatological table fellowship before God. As the messianic Son of man that he is and that he shortly confesses himself to be before the high priest (cf. Mark 14:61–62), he no longer merely wants to reaffirm the Sinai covenant with his blood of the covenant. Rather he wants to induct "the many" at this time into the messianic table fellowship (following the textual relationship that Isa 24:13 and 25:6ff. explicitly establishes with Exod 24:9ff.), corresponding eschatologically with the meal on Sinai, and thus depict its eschatological fulfillment (Luke 22:16). As in the case of the bread saying, so the cup saying has to do with gaining and conveying new life in the correlation of events. Because "all drink from the cup" (Mark 14:23) they obtain a share in the atoning death of Jesus, the power of which reconciles and unites them with God again. Their place at the messianic meal is being prepared when, at peace with God and with those at table with them, they may begin to sing the hymn of thanksgiving from Isaiah 26:1ff. The formulation of the saying concerning the cup is incredibly terse and yet in each individual case is original, meaningful, and significant. It requires no literary correction and decomposition, although it does call for meticulous exegetical examination. If the cup saying is allowed to retain its original wording, the paralleling of the saying concerning the bread and the cup in Mark can hardly be the issue.

It is not surprising but quite understandable that the early Christian teachers and tradents, including the evangelists, endeavored to highlight the full meaning of the cup saying as clearly and unequivocally as possible. Matthew has an addition to the Markan text: "For this is my blood of the covenant which is poured out for many for the forgiveness of sins" (Matt 26:28). For Matthew this clarification is significant (cf. the relationship between Matt 1:21 and 26:28) and in terms of its content is fully justified. The goal of the atoning event that God set in motion through Jesus is indeed the forgiveness of sins.

The Lukan and Pauline texts interpret even more pointedly. Both are traced back to the proto-Lukan passion tradition that was likely native to Antioch.[12] With the extensive realm of missions in mind in which they are to become effective, they establish that the cup Jesus took was the third cup of the four prescribed in the Passover handed "after the meal." The attempt to expose a particular type of meal in contrast to Mark and Matthew from this catechetically motivated explanation is erroneous; we know nothing at all of an early Christian Lord's Supper in which the bread was taken at the beginning and the cup only after the satisfying meal.[13] But the continuing catechetical interpretation is concerned not only with the external

---

[12] On this proto-Lukan tradition, see esp. Joachim Jeremias, *Die Sprache des Lukasevangeliums* (MeyerK; Göttingen: Vandenhoeck & Ruprecht, 1980) 286–323; idem, *New Testament Theology: The Proclamation of Jesus* (trans. John Bowden; New York: Scribner's 1971) 39–41; and Vincent Taylor, *The Passion Narrative of St. Luke* (ed. O. E. Evans; Cambridge: Cambridge University Press, 1972).

[13] K. T. Kleinknecht has pointed out to me (and the participants in the seminar on the Lord's Supper texts that I conducted together with him in the winter semester 1985/86) that Bornkamm's argument, based on the *meta to deipnēsai* in 1 Cor 11:25, in his classical essay, "Lord's Supper and Church in Paul," *Early Christian Experience* (trans. Paul L. Hammer; London: SCM, 1969) 123–60, according to which "an old practice of the celebration, probably no longer demanded by Paul himself, in which bread- and cup-action, bread- and cup-word, were separated by the common meal" (142), lacks any historical documentation in the realm of early Christian tradition. This is nothing but a construct of exegetical investigation based on three Greek words intended to clarify for Diaspora converts without basic Jewish instruction which cup Jesus used in his cup-related action. The only verified meal celebrations in which bread- and cup-action were separated in the manner indicated by Bornkamm are the Passover meal and the Jewish festival meal (the sequence of which is described in detail in Str-B IV/2, 611–39). But because both 1 Cor 11:23–25 and Luke 22:14–20 are traced back to the proto-Lukan passion narrative, *meta to deipnēsai* can hardly point to any meal but the farewell Passover that Jesus celebrated with the Twelve "in the night when Jesus was betrayed."

ity of the cup given "after the meal." The Pauline and Lukan tradition deals explicitly with the question, arising from the Markan and Matthean version, of what kind of covenant is intended when Jesus, the Messiah, sheds his blood of the covenant in correspondence with Exodus 24:8. Their response is thoroughly relevant biblically: It is the new covenant according to Jeremiah 31:31ff., which is opened up through Jesus' vicarious yielding up of his life (i.e., by means of his blood). Hence the word concerning the cup in the Pauline text: "This cup is the new covenant in my blood" (1 Cor 11:25) and in Luke, nuanced even more clearly: "This cup is the new covenant in my blood which is poured out for you" (Luke 22:20).

With this formulation the Pauline and Lukan tradition continues the account of Mark 14:23–24 in a meaningful way and avoids the misunderstanding—a reprehensible one to Jewish ears in light of Leviticus 17:10–11—that Jesus called upon those at table with him at the farewell meal to drink his own blood. For Jewish and Gentile Christians the Lukan and Pauline form of the word concerning the cup is much less offensive and easier to grasp than the Markan and Matthean version. From the history-of-missions perspective, therefore, this tradition proves to be a distinct continuance and further development of Jesus' saying concerning the cup contained in Mark, a saying retained from the apostles' reminiscence, pregnant with symbolism, old and offensive.

It is hardly comprehensible, as frequently assumed, that in the course of the transmission the Pauline/Lukan tradition was changed into the more difficult Markan/Matthean version, which is also more prone to misunderstanding. From the beginning Jeremiah 31:31ff. has not been linked with either the blood of the covenant or the cup and the messianic meal. Both of these follow only from Exodus 24:8ff. and Isaiah 24:13; 25:6ff., hence from Mark. Because in 1 Corinthians 10:16–17 Paul also reveals familiarity with the Markan tradition of institution (see below), everything in the history of tradition favors moving forward from the Markan text to the Pauline/Lukan, rather than vice versa.

In the farewell Passover Jesus' saying concerning the cup too is followed by a series of discourses with his disciples. After

they are completed and the disciples, together with Jesus, drink
the fourth cup of the Passover and sing the second part (Pss
115–118) of the Hallel (Mark 14:26), they go out to the Mount
of Olives, to Gethsemane. The reason Jesus does not go to Beth-
any, as he customarily did (cf. Mark 11:11b par.), but spends the
night in the garden of Gethsemane, is that the night of the
Passover had to be spent in the region of the city of Jerusalem,
according to the regulation already mentioned (cf. Deut 16:5–
7). In order to provide more space for the crowds of pilgrims,
the city limits were extended to the western slope of the Mount
of Olives, where Gethsemane was situated, for the night of the
Passover.[14] Thus it is possible for Judas, who evidently knows
Jesus' intention, to hand Jesus over to the temple guards (Mark
14:32ff. par.).

The Thanksgiving Meal of the Resurrected One

I still have not reached the early Christian celebration of
the Lord's Supper; I have only recounted and traced what Jesus
said and did at the farewell meal in Jerusalem. Yet precisely this
recounting is of crucial significance. From the beginning of the
Christian church the celebration of the Lord's Supper has in no
way been determined by the occasions of Jesus' table fellowship
with tax collectors and sinners, but by his symbolic action
during the farewell meal "in the night in which he was betrayed"
(1 Cor 11:23). Today one still has no decisive reason to depart
from this tradition. One cannot simply identify the private
farewell meal with the Twelve and the public occasions of Jesus'
table fellowship with the tax collectors and sinners. Only after
Easter, as a result of two new and important steps, did the early
Christian Lord's Supper celebration come about in the tradition
in which we continue to celebrate the Lord's Supper today. The

---

[14] Cf. Jeremias, *Eucharistic*, 37 n. 4 and 49–50. Given these measures I
consider David Flusser's assumption to be erroneous that after Gethsemane
Jesus withdrew because "he suspected the danger threatening him and hence
left Jerusalem to escape in the desert," *Die letzten Tage Jesu in Jerusalem* (trans.
H. Zechner; Stuttgart: Calwer, 1982) 82.

first of these steps was associated with Jesus himself, the crucified and resurrected Lord; the second was taken by the disciples,
who awakened to faith and new obedience from their despair
and anguish.

The well-known story of Jesus' two disciples journeying to
Emmaus on Easter (Luke 24:13–35), as well as John 21, graphically tell about the move of the resurrected one toward the
disciples. Both instances deal with Jesus himself, who in new life
appears to the disciples at a meal. The disciples are disillusioned
and, in the case of John 21, have returned to Galilee; by breaking
bread and giving it to them, Jesus receives them anew into the
fellowship (Luke 24:30; John 21:13) that had been shattered by
their defection (Mark 14:50) and despair (Luke 24:21). With the
appearance meals at Emmaus and at the shore of the Sea of
Galilee Jesus turns his disciples afresh into those sharing at table
with him, renews the fellowship of peace with them, and awak-
ens in their hearts the faith of Easter (cf. also Acts 10:40–41).
This Easter experience of reconciliation also causes Peter, John,
and their companions to view in a new light the farewell meal
that they celebrated together on the eve of the Passover in
Jerusalem.

On the evening of Maundy Thursday the eyes and minds
of the Twelve had been occupied with ignorance and perhaps
with fear regarding Jesus' announcement of death. Only hours
later the night of unbelief overtook the entire band of disciples.
Since the risen one appeared, however, and through the new
table fellowship of Easter with him the meaning of Jesus' words
and deeds at the Last Supper, so pregnant with symbolism,
became clear. The Lord had desired to point them beyond the
commemoration of the exodus from Egypt and the making of
the covenant at Sinai that was customarily part of the Jewish
Passover. Through his atoning death he desired to open up for
them the messianic table fellowship before the throne of God and
the communion with God in the new covenant (Jer 31:31ff.). By
means of his appearance at the meal in Emmaus and at the Sea
of Galilee he resumed the table fellowship with his disciples,
who were weak in faith, and thereby authenticated for the first
and decisive time the covenant of peace, for the inauguration of

which he had shed his blood. From now on celebrating the meal of faith meant being the table companion of Jesus, the crucified and resurrected Lord, in remembrance of his passion and in the joy of his resurrection.

Quite logically the apostles now gave this meal a new name and new value. Thereby they took the second important step to which I referred: The meal alongside the resurrected Lord they now called the "meal of the Lord" (1 Cor 11:20), which at the same time gained the splendor of the joy of Easter. In the Lord's meal the disciples did not simply resume the former table fellowship with Jesus, but they celebrated the meal in remembrance of his death and on the basis of his resurrection by God. In keeping with the deep-rooted Jewish custom of celebrating salvation from the throes of death with a meal of thanksgiving, they now understood and celebrated the Lord's Supper as a meal of thanksgiving of the resurrected one.[15] He is the Lord who,

---

[15] Cf. Hartmut Gese, "Psalm 22 und das Neue Testament: Der älteste Bericht vom Tode Jesu und die Entstehung des Herrenmahls," *Vom Sinai zum Zion: Alttestamentliche Beiträge zur biblischen Theologie*, 2d ed. (Munich: Kaiser, 1984) 180–201; and idem, "The Origin of the Lord's Supper," *Essays on Biblical Theology* (trans. Keith Crim; Minneapolis: Augsburg, 1981) 117–40. In view of the Johannine tradition and, in contrast to me, Gese does not consider the synoptic account of Jesus' farewell Passover to be reliable; hence he speaks only by way of suggestion: "The Lord's Supper was Jesus' last meal on earth and was observed in anticipation of the heavenly meal. It thus forms an analogy," "Origin," 127. As understandable (and problematic) as such caution might be, I consider Gese's following statements to be appropriate and directive: "The Lord's Supper is the thank offering *(todah)* of the One who is risen. When we approach the death and resurrection of Jesus in the light of our understanding of the institution of *todah* we would expect to find the *todah* as the worship appropriate to the event of the resurrection, the deliverance of Jesus from death. Biblical thinking would indicate that the new beginning of Jesus' life from death, the Easter event of deliverance, would take the form of a thanksgiving meal. Here Easter occurs for the followers of Jesus as fellowship with Jesus in a meal and participation in Jesus' sacrifice—the participation in the one delivered and in the deliverance," "Origin," 134. The arguments adduced by Jeremias against Gese's view (cf. Jeremias, "Ist das Dankopfermahl der Ursprung des Herrenmahls," *Donum Gentilicium: New Testament Studies in Honour of David Daube* (ed. C. K. Barrett, E. Bammel, and W. D. Davies; Oxford: Clarendon, 1978) 64–67, are not entirely valid considering the multilayered traditions in m. *Pesaḥ.* 2:5 and t. *Ḥag.* 1:6. As Gese told me (by word of mouth), in some editions of t. *Ḥag.* 1:6 the presentation of offerings of thanksgiving at the Matzoth festival is affirmed explicitly on behalf of Rabbi Eleazar ben Rabbi

handed over by his foes to die but marvelously saved out of death by God, himself sets his table (cf. Luke 22:30), the "table of the Lord" (1 Cor 10:21). This meal of thanksgiving was no longer celebrated only once a year (as was the Passover), but on every Sunday as the day of the resurrection (cf. Acts 20:7) and even daily (Acts 2:46). The remembrance now was no longer merely of the deliverance of the former people of God from slavery in Egypt, as commonly practiced in the Jewish meal of thanksgiving and exemplified by Jesus in the farewell Passover, but also and primarily of the passion and resurrection of Jesus. Both aspects were seen as promising realization of the redemption of the new people of God whom Jesus had begun to gather and of which "the believers" (Acts 2:44) considered themselves part because they were linked with the apostles.

The focus of those at table was at the same time not merely retrospectively on the exodus and on Jesus' suffering and death. Prompted by Jesus' eschatological view (cf. Mark 14:25 par.) and blessed by the resurrection of the Lord, the focus was also prospectively on the return of Jesus and the eschatological dawn of God's reign with the messianic table fellowship on Mount Zion. Acts 2:46 refers to the life and celebration of the meal, the *pars pro toto* so called (breaking of bread; cf. also 20:7, 11) of the earliest community in Jerusalem: "And day by day, attending the temple together and breaking bread in their homes, they partook of food with glad and generous hearts." First Corinthians 16:22 also preserves for us the ancient Aramaic prayer voiced at this Lord's Supper: "Maranatha," which means "Our Lord, come!" (referring, of course, to the eschatological coming of Jesus to judge the world and to redeem the people of God).

In the Christian sense of the term, therefore, the Lord's Supper is not merely a Christian form of the Passover meal, nor does it arise simply from Jesus' gatherings at table with tax collectors and sinners. But in view of Jesus' death and resurrection, it is concerned with the meal of thanksgiving for the resurrected Lord who bids the believers to the table fellowship.

Simeon; cf. the edition of Mose S. Zuckermandel (Trier: 1881; reprint, 3d ed. [Jerusalem: 1963]) 233 line 8. Léon-Dufour, *Sharing*, 40–45, 54, 177, concurs with Gese's references.

Because those at table partake of Jesus' vicarious death and new life in, with, and under bread and wine, they are incorporated into the community of Jesus as the vanguard of the new people of God. At this time in Jerusalem the Lord's Supper is the decisive point of crystallization, linking the believers together as the community of Christ.

THE LORD'S SUPPER IN CORINTH

First Corinthians 10:15–17 and 11:17–34 indicate how the communities established by Paul were supposed to—and did— celebrate the Lord's Supper under his guidance. In 1 Corinthians 11:17–34 Paul has to call the Corinthians to order because there were abuses in their celebration of the Lord's Supper. So as to bring matters into line again, he reminds them of the instructions he had previously given them for the communal celebration of the meal:

> For I received from the Lord what I also handed on to you, that the Lord Jesus on the night when he was betrayed took a loaf of bread, and when he had given thanks, he broke it and said, "This is my body that is for you. Do this in remembrance of me." In the same way he took the cup also, after supper, saying, "This cup is the new covenant in my blood. Do this, as often as you drink it, in remembrance of me." For as often as you eat this bread and drink the cup, you proclaim the Lord's death until he comes (NRSV).

In terms of the history of tradition, one can explain the remarkable agreement between the Pauline Lord's Supper text and the Lukan account in that in his missions catechesis, among other things, Paul begins with an antecedent form of the Lukan passion narrative commonly used in the mission to the Gentiles. Paul became acquainted with this tradition of the passion (which in part also emerges, e.g., in 1 Cor 2:6ff.)[16] in Antioch (or in

---

[16] Apart from 1 Cor 2:8 no NT text speaks more clearly of the "rulers," ignorant of his divine majesty and function, who crucified Jesus than Acts 3:17. *Hoi archontes* is Luke's standard designation for the Jewish members of the

Damascus?), adopted it as authoritative tradition, and henceforth passed it on as such. Thus his claim that he received the Lord's Supper *paradosis* "from the Lord" and passed on the tradition (1 Cor 11:23) is not fiction but affords a glimpse into the early Christian-Pauline missions catechesis. The words of institution, of which Paul reminds readers in 1 Corinthians 11:23–25, belong to the tradition that in Antioch has been traced back to Jesus himself via the tradents.[17]

Yet much more important than this intriguing tradition-historical state of affairs are the emphases Paul established for the celebration of the meal. These are essentially twofold: First, the Lord's Supper ought to and will be a meal of participation; second, the proclamation of the death of Jesus is to be central to this meal until he comes (again).

Paul places utmost emphasis on the key word *participation*. In 1 Corinthians 10:16–17 he writes: "The cup of blessing which we bless, is it not a participation in the body of Christ? Because there is one bread, we who are many are one body, for we all partake of the one bread." The form and manner of expression in these statements indicate that the apostle here likewise links up with didactic tradition that was already known in Corinth. The key terms "breaking bread" and "participation" in the *paradosis* point to Acts 2:42, 46, while "bless," "blood of Christ," and "the many" interestingly point to Mark 14:22–24.[18]

Sanhedrin and officials (cf. Luke 14:1; 23:13, 35; 24:20; Acts 3:17; 4:5, 8, 26 [including a quotation from Ps 2:2]; 13:27). From this point of reference a connection in the history of tradition between 1 Cor 2:8 and the Lukan tradition is likely. In addition 1 Cor 15:3–11 is nowhere illustrated better than in Luke 23 and 24 and in Acts. If the traditions Luke adopted in his Gospel and in Acts were native especially to Antioch, one can easily assume Paul's knowledge of these traditions.

[17] Thus the chain of tradents runs from Jesus via the original apostles (Peter, John, etc.), to the so-called hellenists and from them to the community in Antioch. In the case of the tradition of the Lord's Supper the path takes one from Jesus to the Jerusalem passion tradition, especially as preserved in Mark, and from there to the proto-Lukan passion narrative from which the Pauline text in 1 Cor 11:23ff. is derived. (With the Markan perspective in mind, Luke then revised this tradition once more in the composition of his Gospel.)

[18] The relationship of tradition described briefly in nn. 16, 17 above poses no problem for the concurrent knowledge of (proto-) Markan and (proto-) Lukan traditions of the passion and the Lord's Supper in Paul.

One learns from 1 Corinthians 10:16–17 that for the apostle the words of institution, cited in 11:23–25, mean more than merely the identification of wine and bread with the blood and body of Jesus and the eating of the same. For Paul, the issue of the Lord's Supper is that those at table share in Jesus—in the fruit of his atoning death, in the power of his bodily resurrection, and in the hope, predicated upon Jesus' death and resurrection, of the eschatological coming of Jesus to redeem and to judge. In the celebration of the Lord's Supper the history and person of Jesus are to be the power shaping the life of faith of those at table. By means of the spiritual drink and the spiritual food that the community takes, like Israel in the exodus from Egypt (1 Cor 10:3–4), by means of the communal eating of the bread and the communal drinking of "the cup of the Lord" (1 Cor 10:21; 11:28) at the "table of the Lord" (1 Cor 10:21), "the many" for whom Jesus died are united in the community of Jesus Christ, that is, in Paul's terminology, in the "body of Christ" (1 Cor 12:12ff.; Rom 12:4ff.). All of them share in the vicarious sacrifice of his person (i.e., in his body), in the atoning power of his death (i.e., in the new covenant opened up by virtue of the atoning effectiveness of the blood of Jesus), and in the Holy Spirit as the presence and mode of operation of the resurrected one (1 Cor 10:3–4; 12:13). The communion with Jesus, the reconciler and Lord, accords with the communion of the members of the community, symbolized in being at table together. At the "table of the Lord," prepared by the resurrected Lord himself, the many become and are (his) one body (1 Cor 10:17; 12:12–13).[19]

For Paul this experience of participation is not merely a process taking place in the recesses of believers' hearts; rather it is of crucial importance to him that the outward form of the

---

[19] In view of the symbolic meaning of the one cup from which all drink who partake of the meal (see n. 9 above), and the ecclesiological meaning of the Lord's Supper already given in Jerusalem, the Pauline correlation of the crucified body of Jesus, the Lord's Supper, and the body-of-Christ concept is free of the abstruse "passion mysticism" that Käsemann suspects when the body of Jesus, offered for us on the cross (cf. 1 Cor 11:24; Rom 7:4), is correlated directly with the Pauline concept of the church as body of Christ (cf. E. Käsemann, "The Theological Problem Presented by the Motif of the Body of Christ," *Perspectives on Paul* [trans. Margaret Kohl; Philadelphia: Fortress, 1971] 111–12).

Lord's Supper celebration accords with the communion of Jesus with his table guests, which is in the process of becoming a reality in that celebration, as well as with the communion of the guests among themselves. A Lord's Supper celebration that is not a visible expression of participation in Christ and in life is worthless, according to Paul. In 1 Corinthians 11:17–31 he drives this home unambiguously to the Corinthians.

When Paul founded the church in Corinth he probably introduced the following form of the Lord's Supper celebration.[20] The members of the community gather for the Lord's Supper at least every Sunday (1 Cor 16:2), perhaps even more frequently. The Lord's meal is celebrated (as in Jerusalem and Antioch) as a full community meal. Everyone contributed their affordable share in food and drink for this meal; it is a matter of course that those who were poorer and the destitute were allowed to eat their fill of the foods presented as much as the more prosperous members of the community. The leader of the community gave a brief or longer address preceding the communal celebration of the meal. (Paul very likely understood his first letter to the Corinthians to be an exhortation from which a reading was to be given in the gathered community prior to the Lord's Supper celebration. The reading then led to the celebration of the meal. The conclusion of the letter still reflects this transition to the Lord's Supper quite clearly.)[21]

The celebration of the meal itself (probably) took the following shape. Those at the meal greeted and accepted one another with the holy kiss and the one in charge of the celebration spoke the benediction: "The grace of the Lord Jesus be with you! If anyone does not love the Lord, let that person be ac-

---

[20] I base the following reconstruction on an overall view of 1 Cor 11:17–34; 16:19–24; and Did. 9:1–5, considering the consistency in the liturgical instructions. Only the liturgical understanding (over against 1 Cor 11:23–26) of the inverted sequence of cup and bread in 1 Cor 10:16 (and identically in Did. 9:2–4) provides the necessary base for the ecclesial interpretation of 1 Cor 10:16–17, e.g., in Ernst Käsemann, "The Pauline Doctrine of the Lord's Supper," *Essays on New Testament Themes* (trans. W. J. Montague, SBT 1/41; Naperville, Ill: Allenson, 1964) 110.

[21] Cf. Günther Bornkamm, "On the Understanding of Worship, B: the Early Christian Lord's Supper Liturgy," *Early Christian Experience*, 169–76.

cursed!" (cf. 1 Cor 16:20–23 with Did. 9:5). Then the praise or prayer of thanksgiving was spoken over the wine to be drunk later on, and the same was practiced regarding the bread to be distributed during the meal (cf. 1 Cor 10:16–17 with Did. 9:1–4). But neither was distributed yet; rather the satiating main course was eaten first. Only at the end of the main course were bread and wine distributed, following the text of 1 Corinthians 11:23–26, in the order of the bread first and then the cup, "after the meal." The prayer for the eschatological coming of the Lord, which the early community preserved in Aramaic in 1 Corinthians 16:22 (also attested for the Lord's Supper celebration in Did. 10:6), "Maranatha," concluded the meal. If Paul himself was present, he led the gathering (cf. Acts 20:7ff.); if he was not, one of the "overseers" likely did (one may assume that those mentioned in Phil 1:1 were in Corinth as well). Because this was a communal meal, all the members of the community participated in it (cf. 1 Cor 12:13). Excluded were only the unbelievers, "who did not love the Lord" (1 Cor 16:22). For Paul, too, the Lord's Supper was not the public meal with tax collectors and sinners, but (analogous to Exod 12:43ff.) the meal of those recognizing Jesus as their reconciler and Lord. On the whole the celebration of the Lord's Supper was shaped by the "remembrance" of Jesus, mentioned twice in the Pauline text, and by the proclamation of his salvific death "until he comes" (1 Cor 11:26).

The phrase "in remembrance of me," which already appears in Luke 22:19, refers to the Christian parallel to the remembrance of the exodus that determined the Jewish Passover celebration, and to the saving acts of God following the Passover (cf. Exod 12:14; 13:3–10; Deut 16:3; Jub. 49:15).[22] But because the remembrance observed in the Lord's Supper took its orientation from Jesus' farewell meal "in the night in which he was betrayed" (cf. 1 Cor 11:23b with Rom 4:25; 8:32) and the Lord's Supper was celebrated as a meal of thanksgiving of the resurrected one, the Lord's Supper remembrance no longer draws exclusively from the commemoration of Israel's redemption

---

[22] Cf. Ferdinand Hahn, "Herrengedächtnis und Herrenmahl bei Paulus," *Exegetische Beiträge*, 304–5.

from slavery in Egypt. Instead it draws its life from the remembrance of Jesus' passion as the suffering and anguish of death. Out of this death God delivered his Son by the resurrection and through this death he brought about redemption for the new people of God. This opens up a broad salvation-history scope for the phrase "in remembrance of me." It extends from the exodus event, via the ancients' experiences on the journey through the wilderness (cf. 1 Cor 10:1–13), to the cross—from Israel's initial deliverance to the eschatological redemption on Golgotha (cf. Rom 3:24–26). The likelihood is considerable that the Lord's Supper remembrance and the proclamation of Jesus' death until the Parousia took the form of reciting and interpreting the passion narrative.[23] The remembrance and petition for the exalted Lord to "come" and for his God-given messianic work of salvation to be completed with his return are linked directly with Luke 22:15, 28–30; Mark 14:25; 14:61–62. In the Lord's Supper the death of Jesus is proclaimed as an event of redemption and promise.

First Corinthians 11:17–34 indicates that unfortunately the Corinthians did not adhere to the ordering of the Lord's Supper just described. Some in the community formed groups that looked down upon the others and that rivaled one another theologically. They came up against one another again at the Lord's Supper (cf. 1 Cor 11:18–19 with 1:10ff.). Because influential individuals in the community considered eating bread and wine at the conclusion of the Lord's Supper to be much more important than the mutual participation of all, as expressed in the community meal as a whole,[24] they began the

---

[23] Etienne Trocmé locates the *Sitz im Leben* of the oldest passion narrative in "the liturgical commemoration of Christ's death by Christians during the Jewish Passover celebration," *The Passion as Liturgy* (London: SCM, 1983) 82. Just as one cannot rule out a usage such as this of the passion narrative in Jerusalem and other Jewish-Christian communities, so the institution of the *todah*, the anamnesis formula in Luke 22:19 which is supported by the passion tradition, 1 Cor 11:24–25 and the Pauline "as often as" in 1 Cor 11:26 suggest that one consider a regular recitation of the passion texts to be linked with the celebration of the Lord's Supper.

[24] On this matter see the fine treatment by Bornkamm, "Lord's Supper and Church in Paul," *Early Christian Experience*, 127–29, 146–47.

meal before everybody had gathered together in order to still their hunger. Accordingly, the poor (e.g., the slaves and laborers who were not able readily to take time off as they wished) went without food (1 Cor 11:22).

Paul criticizes all this firmly and decisively: It is scandalous for the community to gather together for the Lord's Supper only so that the old groups and parties can meet again. It is equally offensive for members of the community not to wait for one another to eat but instead to devour the food they brought before the Lord's Supper. In this case hardly anything is left for the (poorer) members of the community who arrive later. They have to celebrate the Lord's table with hunger pangs and with those at table who are satiated and possibly already inebriated. Paul denounces this: "When you meet together, it is not the Lord's Supper that you eat. For in eating, each one goes ahead with his own meal, and one is hungry and another is drunk. What! Do you not have houses to eat and drink in? Or do you despise the church of God and humiliate those who have nothing? What shall I say to you? Shall I commend you in this? No, I will not" (1 Cor 11:20–22).

Paul writes that this activity in Corinth has to cease at once: "So then, my brothers and sisters, when you come together to eat, wait for one another—if any one is hungry, let that one eat at home—lest you come together to be condemned. About the other things I will give directions when I come" (1 Cor 11:33–34). In the community all begin to eat at the same time and eat together, else the Lord's Supper turns into a meal of judgment for the community. The Lord's Supper is not the place for feasting and drinking among those who are like-minded. One must carefully distinguish between the bread to satisfy hunger and the body of the Lord, between table beverage to quench thirst and the cup of salvation. All have to know at whose table they are invited, and table manners and table talk are to correspond. The topics at the table of the Lord are Jesus' redemptive death, mutual acceptance, and the hope of the Parousia. Those wanting a different practice—disregarding the poorer members of the community and despising the companions at the Lord's table who think differently—take upon themselves the wrath of Jesus, indeed of Jesus as the judge on judgment day!

If we have read it correctly, the warning, "If anyone does not love the Lord [Christ], let him be accursed!" (1 Cor 16:22), was pronounced already in Corinth at the outset of the celebration of the meal (as later on in Did. 9:5; 10:6). Paul was altogether serious about this warning when he wrote:

> Whoever, therefore, eats the bread or drinks the cup of the Lord in an unworthy manner will be answerable for the body and blood of the Lord. Examine yourselves, and only then eat of the bread and drink of the cup. For all who eat and drink without discerning the body [of Christ from the satiating bread], eat and drink judgment against themselves (1 Cor 11:30–31, NRSV).

For Paul those who sit at Jesus' table and want forgiveness of sins only for themselves, without drawing any consequences for their interpersonal conduct, have the same experience as did the so-called unmerciful servant in Jesus' parable in Matthew 18:23–35. In Jesus' favor and in the forgiveness he receives, he collects the judgment.

The apostle is upset that not a few among the Corinthians eat the bread of life and drink the cup of salvation carelessly, and declares: "that is why many of you are weak and ill, and some have died. But if we judged ourselves truly, we should not be judged." At the Lord's Supper those at table with Jesus are highly exalted and share in a peace that they cannot grant themselves. But if they neglect to become peacemakers themselves on the basis of this gift of peace (cf. Rom 12:18 with Matt 5:9), they also fail gravely. Because Jesus is near in the celebration of the meal, it is possible in his presence to obtain not only forgiveness of sins and new life but also death, if one disregards the love of the Lord and his instruction.

Under the imprint of this warning by Paul the ancient church (beginning with Justin) practiced the community meal and the Lord's Supper celebration separately.

THE JOHANNINE MEAL TRADITION

To examine the totality of the biblical tradition of the Lord's Supper, I now also need to direct attention to the text tradition of John 6:52–58, which I have mentioned only briefly, and to the perspective from which the Fourth Gospel views the Lord's Supper.

It is wise to begin the consideration of the Johannine text by acknowledging two presuppositions. In terms of the history of tradition and of early Christianity it is more probable that the Gospel of John was written in view of the Markan and Lukan tradition, rather than without any knowledge or entirely separate from the entire synoptic tradition.[25] This analysis must also be guided by the final form of the Gospel as handed down and the forms of the text offered in it. As John 21 indicates with particular clarity, this Gospel was subject to the redaction of the "Johannine circle" (which has its say indirectly in 21:24–25). As much as this observation favors the assumption of internal growth of the Johannine tradition, it is equally difficult to show this growth process convincingly in terms of literary criticism and redaction. Not least does this difficulty apply to the analysis of chapters 6 and 13, which are particularly important for the topic at hand.

To understand the Lord's Supper tradition in the Johannine context, it is important to keep in mind that the tradition of Jesus' farewell Passover meal with the Twelve changed soon after Easter into the liturgy of the Lord's Supper as "the *todah* of the risen one," hence that the early Christian Lord's Supper became detached from the Passover date. The situation in Paul, where 1 Corinthians 10:16–17 is based on the Markan tradition and 1 Corinthians 11:23ff. on the (proto-) Lukan Lord's Supper tradition, indicates that these two versions of the text had no essential difference of content. In a context of argumentation, contrasting the new existence and behavior of the community with their preconversion conduct and existence, Paul is further-

---

[25] Cf. C. K. Barrett, *The Gospel According to St. John* (2d ed.; London: SPCK, 1978) 42ff. In the realm of tradition of the OT, early Judaism, and early Christianity the preceding traditions generally are not simply pushed aside, disposed of, and criticized, but rather continued and heightened. In this sense Léon-Dufour, *Sharing*, 251, is correct: "All this does not mean, however, that John disparages the sacrament, for in his own way he gives the equivalent of the synoptic texts. . . . His special contribution is to make known the real and abiding meaning of the Eucharist."

more able to remind the Corinthians that "a little leaven leavens the whole lump." He continues: "Cleanse out the old leaven that you may be a new lump, as you really [already] are unleavened. For Christ, our paschal lamb, has been sacrificed. Let us, therefore, celebrate the festival, not with the old leaven, the leaven of malice and evil, but with the unleavened bread of sincerity and truth" (1 Cor 5:6–8).

For the apostle, therefore, it was entirely feasible to link the knowledge of the proto-Lukan tradition of the passion with the seemingly very Johannine observation that Christ died as "our Passover lamb," as the Christians' true Passover lamb, and that for the community, therefore, the time of the eschatological redemption (and of their corresponding behavior) had begun (cf. also Rom 3:24–25). In view of this linking of traditions in Paul one ought to be inclined toward a manner of observation that is as inclusive as possible, rather than toward an exclusive or alternative one with reference to the Gospel of John.

As already mentioned, on account of its particular chronology of the passion, and unlike the Synoptics, the Fourth Gospel is not able to speak of an institution of the Lord's Supper in the framework of the farewell Passover meal. Yet interestingly the structure and content of John 13 demonstrate that Luke 22 is reflected even to the point of the sequence of scenes in the account of Jesus' farewell meal, in the foot washing, as well as in the following identification of the betrayer.[26] As Joachim Jeremias has already observed, John 13:10 furthermore indicates that the Johannine account is based on a narrative tradition that understood Jesus' farewell meal as a Passover meal.[27] The term "bathed" in 13:10 refers to the regulation that those partaking in the Passover meal were to do so in purity and hence had to submit themselves to a prior dip-bath (cf. Josephus, *J. W.*

---

[26] This emerges clearly from the synopsis offered in Karl Theodor Kleinknecht's essay, "Johannes 13, die Synoptiker und die 'Methode' der johanneischen Evangelienüberlieferung," *ZTK* 82 (1985) 370–71. Kleinknecht's main argument makes sense: "John 13 can be retraced as a productive rereading of Mark 14 (Matt 26) and Luke 22, as a fresh narration of the tradition which refers to the latter without becoming dependent upon it" (384).

[27] Cf. Jeremias, *Eucharistic*, 79–84.

6:425–26 and m. Pesaḥ. 8:5, 8; 9:1). Likewise the identification of the betrayer by means of the dipped piece of bread in John 13:26 finds its simplest explanation in the custom of dipping and eating green herbs and lettuce in vinegar or in a fruit-and-nut mixture during the preliminary course of the Passover.

In his mind John does not alter the (synoptic-Lukan) tradition given to him; in the presentation of Jesus' farewell meal he omits the words of institution and moves to center stage the foot-washing scene, as well as the commandment to love one another that arises from it. Hence for the Johannine community too this meal is very significant. The servant act of washing the feet carried out by Jesus signifies that the disciples become "clean all over" (13:10) in that Jesus suffers death for them and his blood cleanses the believers from all sin (1 John 1:7). From Jesus' ministry, which is a ministry of love (John 13:1; 15:13–14; 1 John 4:9–10), a twofold obligation arises for the disciples. First and foremost is the obligation to love one another (13:34), which, as already indicated in Mark 10:41–45 and Luke 22:24–30, is intended as the characteristic of the Johannine community, inwardly as well as outwardly (cf. John 13:35 with 1 John 3:23–24). At the same time, however, in view of the example of Jesus (cf. John 13:15 with Luke 22:27) the disciples are to be clear about the fact that an apostle commissioned by Jesus cannot and should not be more than the serving Lord who commissioned him (John 13:16; cf. with 17:18; 20:21–23; and Matt 10:24 par.). For this reason a devaluation of the Lord's Supper tradition in John is out of the question, although the institution of the Lord's Supper, which is central to this meal even in Luke, has been replaced by the foot washing in John.

The reasons for this substitution do not seem to be to devalue or even to relinquish the early Christian meal of the Lord. Rather the close terminological associations of John 6:51b and 52–58 with the early Christian tradition of the Lord's Supper allow for the conclusion that John unfolds in chapter 6 how he wants the Lord's Supper to be valued and viewed. John 6:51b corresponds most closely with the (proto-) Lukan-Pauline saying concerning the bread (Luke 22:19; 1 Cor 11:24); Mark 14:24 (Matt 26:28) speaks more clearly about drinking the blood of the Son of man (John 6:53ff.) than the Lukan-Pauline text. The verbs John uses, "to eat" (*phagein*) and "to drink" (*pinein*), appear in the Lord's Supper context both in the Matthean version (Matt 26:26ff.) and in Mark 14:25 par.; Luke 22:15–18; and 1 Cor 11:25–26. The specifically Johannine *trogein*, "eat, chew" (John 6:54ff. and 13:18 in the citation of Ps 41:10), has no parallel in Paul or in the Synoptics; yet Psalm 41:10 is also behind the formulation of Mark 14:18.

Given all this, the eucharistic tenor of John 6:51b and 52–58 is obvious. These verses are formulated with the (proto-) Lukan and Markan Lord's Supper tradition in mind, the influences of which intersect similarly in John 6:51b and 52ff. as they do in 1 Corinthians 10:16–17 and 11:23ff.[28] The Johannine text highlights clearly that, as the Bread of Life having come from heaven, Jesus offers his flesh to be eaten and his blood to be drunk in the Lord's Supper, so that those who receive both may share in eternal life and have the assurance that (as the Son of man) Jesus will raise them on the day of judgment. The clarity with which 6:53ff. speaks of the flesh and blood of Christ as the central essence of the elements of the Lord's Supper surpasses even 1 Corinthians 10:16–17, probably for specific reasons.

Before pursuing these reasons further, one still has to consider whether John 6:51b and 52–58 represent an (ecclesiastical-) redactional addendum to the bread discourse or an authentic part of the text of the discourse and of the composition of chapter 6 as a whole. The wording of the verses accords so closely with the context of the Bread of Life discourse that one must consider them to have been written for the context of John 6 in any case; from the perspective of terminology and content they would have no purpose elsewhere in the Gospel. Hence one must decide the question of whether they are an addendum on the basis of the composition of the Bread of Life discourse and of chapter 6 as a whole.

As for the composition of the chapter as a whole, the sequence shaping the chapter—the feeding narrative, Jesus' walk-

---

[28] Thus Kleinknecht's thesis of a "productive rereading" of the Synoptic tradition (in "Johannes 13") is also confirmed with reference to John 6.

ing on the water, the demand for a sign, the disciples' lack of understanding, and Peter's confession—may have been available to the evangelist via the Markan tradition (cf. John 6:1ff. with Mark 6:32ff. and 8:1ff.; John 6:16ff. with Mark 6:45ff.; John 6:30ff. with Mark 8:11ff.; John 6:60ff. with Mark 8:14ff.; and John 6:66ff. with Mark 8:27ff.). It is John himself who composes and interprets this narratival sequence with a view of and from the starting point of the Bread of Life discourse. In the "sign" of the multiplication of the loaves the sensible reader is to see the feeding of the new people of God, corresponding with Moses' feeding of the ancient people of God in the wilderness (cf. John 6:14 with Exod 16:4ff.; Num 11:10ff.; and Deut 18:18ff.).[29]

In the scene of Jesus' walking on the water, to the eye of faith he proves to be the Son of God who, like God, "trampled the waves of the sea" (Job 9:8). He comes to the disciples, who are threatened by the chaotic powers (of the water), and identifies himself to them as God in person by means of the form of divine self-identification of *egō eimi* (It is I).

In the following Bread of Life discourse (6:22–59) the reader is led to understand Jesus as "the bread from heaven," given and sent by God himself, which satisfies eternally and therein surpasses even the wisdom for which the prudent continually hunger and thirst (cf. 6:35 with Sir 24:21). According to Wisdom 16 the ancient people of God were to learn from the miracle of the manna that the angelic food provided from heaven was a sign of the divine word (*rhēma*) which preserves those trusting in God (*pisteuontes*) better than any earthly nourishment does (Wis 16:26). The Bread of Life discourse teaches those who believe in Jesus (*pisteuontes*) to understand that Jesus is the living bread having come down from heaven, so that everyone who partakes of him receives eternal life. Partaking in Jesus is made concrete by faith in him, by hearing his word and eating the "food" that the Son of man offers in the form of his flesh and blood, in order that those who eat Jesus' flesh and

---

[29] On this typological combination of traditions, see Ferdinand Hahn, "Die alttestamentlichen Motive in der urchristlichen Abendmahl, über lieferung," *EvT* 27 (1967) 349ff.; and idem, "Zum Stand der Erforschung des urchristlichen Herrenmahls," *Exegetische Beiträge*, 250–51.

drink his blood have eternal life and may be confident that Jesus will raise them on the last day (cf. 6:27, 51, 53–54).

According to the Johannine presentation, Jesus' identification with the bread from heaven and the promise of the nourishment leading to eternal life in the form of the flesh and blood of the Son of man are not only offensive to the imprudent Jews who "grumble" and "struggle" against Jesus, just as the ancient people of God grumbled and struggled against Moses (cf. 6:41ff., 52ff.). The Bread of Life discourse in the synagogue of Capernaum (6:59) comes to a point eucharistically in verses 52ff., and for many disciples is likewise an offense of such gravity that they henceforth refuse to follow Jesus and they forsake him (6:60–66). Only the Twelve remain with him. As their spokesman Peter avers that Jesus has "words of eternal life" (*rhēmata zōēs aiōniou*) and that in him they recognized the "Holy One of God," the Messiah (perhaps better: messianic high priest), who is "sealed" (authenticated) by the gift of the Spirit (cf. John 6:69 with 6:27 and 1:33–34, 41, as well as with Ps 106:16).

If one extrapolates John 6:52–58 (or even 6:51b–58) from this overall context, the profundity of the Bread of Life discourse and of the overall composition breaks apart, because the midrashic pattern pointed out by Peder Borgen is mutilated. According to Borgen the citation of Psalm 78:24 in John 6:31 is interpreted in the text that follows, verses 32–46 with reference to the "bread from heaven," and verses 47–58 with reference to "eating." [30] To treat verses 51b–58 as an addendum is to fail to recognize and to truncate this context. The overall composition falls apart because the trajectory from the feeding narrative to the feeding of the believers through Jesus' flesh and blood (cf. 6:11–13 with 6:27, 51, 55) is broken, and the Bread of Life discourse is virtually arrested at an antithetical point. Indeed, it is not the divine word of wisdom that keeps the believers but only faith in the human Jesus as the personified Bread of Heaven. That it is this antithesis that caused "many disciples" to

---

[30] Cf. Peder Borgen, *Bread from Heaven: An Exegetical Study of the Concept of Manna in the Gospel of John and the Writings of Philo* (NovTSup 10; Leiden: Brill, 1965) 59ff.

abandon him (6:60–66) is hard to conceive in the Johannine context, because the confession of the prologue (1:1–18) already leads to the surpassing of the OT wisdom tradition by the revelation of Jesus.[31] But if the offense that "many disciples" are taking in Jesus' discourse also refers specifically to the eucharistic intensification in the Bread of Life discourse in 6:52ff., then 6:52–71 describes an offense that is verifiable in the history of the early church and the rise of a schism in the Johannine circle.

Serious opposition from the Jews arises against the Christian perspective that the Lord's Supper elements are identical with the flesh and blood of Jesus, because the consumption of blood represents a sacrilege punishable by scourging or even extermination (cf. Lev 7:26–27; 17:10ff., as well as m. *Ker.* 1:1; *Tg. Yer. I* on Lev 7:27; m. *Mak.* 3:2). The Johannine circle seems to have been subject to such opposition. That the incarnation of Jesus is made concrete throughout, even in his cruel sacrificial death, and that baptism and the Lord's Supper provided a partaking only in the Jesus from whose wound in the side flowed water and blood (19:34–35), was already contested in the Johannine circle itself, following 1 John 5:6, even to the point of a schism (cf. 1 John 2:18–19, 22ff.; 4:1ff.; 5:5–12). Around AD 120 Ignatius of Antioch laments that Christian heretics "abstain from eucharist and prayer, because they allow not that the eucharist is the flesh of our Savior Jesus Christ, which flesh suffered for our sins, and which the Father of his goodness raised up" (Ign. *Smyrn.* 6:2). According to John 6:52–59 and 60–71 it appears that precisely this situation and debate already began in the Johannine circle. If this view is correct, the Bread of Life discourse takes hold of an acute problem of faith and life in the Johannine community. On account of its understanding of the Lord's Supper, the community is threatened from the outside by the Jewish opposition and from within by the schism. In this situation only those are able to stand firm who are taught by God himself and are born anew by baptism and by experiencing

---

[31] This has also been ignored in Hans Weder's otherwise fine essay continuing the discussion: "Die Menschwerdung Gottes: Überlegungen zur Auslegungsproblematik des Johannesevangeliums am Beispiel von Johannes 6," ZTK 82 (1985) 344ff.

the Spirit, who experience and understand Jesus' words as Spirit-borne and life-giving (cf. John 6:63 with 1:12–13; 3:5–6; 1 John 4:1–14; 5:5–12). In the light of all this it is wise not to intervene in the text of the Bread of Life discourse in John 6 but to take verses 51b and 52–58 as a genuine component of the discourse.

If one views John 13 and John 6, including the disputed verses 51b and 52–58, as I have outlined, the following aspects arise for the Johannine understanding of the Lord's Supper. The substitution of the words of institution with the foot washing in chapter 13 is determined neither merely by the unique Johannine passion chronology, according to which Jesus, as the true Passover lamb, "accomplished" (19:30) his mission on the cross at precisely the hour when the Passover lambs were slaughtered in the temple (1:29; cf. 19:36 with the citation from Exod 12:46); nor does it have anything to do with a Johannine critique of the Lord's Supper. Rather, one finds the reason for the substitution in the confrontation that the Johannine circle faced. One can infer this confrontation from John 6. If one considers the two instances of the future tense in 6:27 and 6:51b: The Son of man "*will* give you the food which endures to eternal life," and "he *will* give [the bread from heaven]" in the form of his flesh sacrificed "for the life of the world," the Lord's Supper emerges as a life-giving gift of Jesus, who completed his mission via incarnation, bestowal of the Spirit in baptism, passion, crucifixion, burial, resurrection, and return to the Father's glory. First John 5:5ff. leads to the same perspective.

Understood correctly the Lord's Supper, for John, is a sacrament of the resurrection, promised by Jesus himself, because it affords sharing in Jesus' flesh and blood, which he yielded up and shed for the life of the world. In John 6:52ff. the Fourth Gospel speaks of the Lord's Supper as a meal that only the resurrected Son of man will and is able to serve, as countermove against Christian pseudofaith (so-called Docetism) that takes offense in Jesus' incarnation, passion, and sacrificial death. The focus on the elements in the Johannine circle's solid understanding of the Lord's Supper was probably a further reason for their distancing from the synagogue community (cf. John 9:22; 12:42; 16:2). What is clear in any case is that the understanding of the Lord's Supper in John 6:51b and 52–58 corresponds quite closely with the early Christian understanding of this meal as the "Lord's Supper" (1 Cor 11:20) presented by the crucified risen one himself at his table.

If one follows the trajectory in John 6, leading from the feeding narrative to 6:52ff., one may further adduce that for the Johannine circle the Lord's Supper is the provision of the true people of God (cf. John 15:1ff.), who fulfill their earthly task as witnesses (16:5–15; 17:14ff.), whom the world is to recognize by their mutual love (13:34–35), and who, in the midst of their tribulation (16:1ff., 33), look forward with anticipation to the resurrection on the last day by the Son of man. This focus too links the Johannine circle with those who proclaim the Lord's death in the context of the Lord's Supper and who pray fervently for his eschatological coming by means of their "Maranatha" (1 Cor 11:26; 16:22).

Following the Johannine understanding, the Son of man, having fulfilled his mission, administers his flesh and blood as food and drink in the Lord's Supper and thus grants his own to share in him as the Bread of Life sent by God. This he grants as the Logos sent by God, who alone has seen the Father; those who are capable of learning from him by the grace of God he assists in understanding and seeing the Father in the Son by means of his word, whereby he grants the Spirit and life (6:44–46, 63). In the Fourth Gospel, as well as in the Johannine letters, one cannot isolate flesh and blood from the knowledge and understanding of the mission and passion of Jesus, and only those who in Jesus have recognized the "Holy One of God," whose words offer eternal life (6:68), are able to partake of the Lord's Supper.

If one sees these correlations, one has no reason to assume that John intended to turn the Lord's Supper into a "medicine of immortality" (Ign. *Eph.* 20:2) by means of his pointed formulations against pseudofaith in 6:53ff. For John the Lord's Supper elements represent the epitomized concretion of the word of God, which Jesus is himself in his self-surrender for the world.[32]

---

[32] In his short catechism of 1535 Johannes Brenz explains the "Supper" of Christ as "a sacrament and divine word-sign (*Wortzeichen*) in which Christ truly offers us his body and blood in his presence and thereby assures us that

As long as John 6 and Jesus' Bread of Life discourse continue to be the framework for 6:52–58, the Johannine words regarding the Lord's Supper also remain protected from sacramental isolation and bias. The sacramental component in John 6:52ff. is no stronger or weaker than in Paul, who traces sickness and death among the Corinthians back to the unworthy eating of the Lord's Supper (1 Cor 11:27ff.). Paul stresses that baptism and the Lord's Supper are no charm against defecting from faith and against sin (1 Cor 10:1–13); John 6:60–71 contains similarly accentuated warnings.

In the second century the so-called Quartodecimans, a Jewish Christian group from Syria and Asia Minor, celebrated the Passover at the same time and in the same manner as did the Jews:

> from the evening of 14th Nisan until three o'clock early on the 15th. . . . But whereas the Jewish evening of festivities was characterized by an atmosphere of happiness until midnight, because they commemorated the nation's liberation from Egyptian bondage, and a particular seriousness commensurate with the matzo festival did not enter in until then, the situation in the celebration of the Quartodecimans was just the converse. Their service began with a fast until midnight and, according to the earliest sources, was held on behalf of the unbelieving Jewish brethren; only then followed the part of the festival characterized by happiness. Its glorious climax was the agape feast and the receiving of the Eucharist.[33]

---

we have the forgiveness of sins and eternal life" (cited in Christoph Weismann, *Eine kleine Biblia: Die Katechismen von Luther und Brenz: Einführung und Texte* [Stuttgart: Calwer, 1985] 115). With regard to the particularly apt expression "catchword" (German *Wortzeichen*) in our context, Weismann remarks that it represents a "concept traceable to the 9th century" from which the term "token" has evolved. He continues: "By the 16th century the old term 'catchword' was already disappearing and only in the South German realm did it continue to be used. Brenz presumably picked the term deliberately because he considered its signification as 'sign, token, proof for the purpose of affirmation and confirmation' to be particularly apt. The same was true of the apparent correlation between word and sign for the essence of the sacrament as a sign confirming and strengthening God's Word and promise" (148 n. 87).

[33] August Strobel, *Ursprung und Geschichte des frühchristlichen Oster-kalenders* (TU 121; Berlin: Akademie, 1977) 17.

The Quartodecimans consistently appealed to the Gospel of John in support of their practice. Indeed, nothing opposes taking John 13 and 6, including the Johannine passion chronology, liturgically, as the Quartodecimans did. To be sure, the insight that in both chapters John begins with a revision of the Lukan and Markan Lord's Supper tradition (and of other narrative catenas) militates against the assumption that one ought to begin with John, rather than with the Synoptics, in reconstructing the history of the Lord's Supper. The Johannine presentation is historically secondary to that of the Synoptics.

CONCLUSION

We are now able to sum up. In the reconstruction we followed the historical data and references in all the extant texts of the Lord's Supper and traced the development of the NT tradition of the Lord's Supper. The biblical tradition of the Lord's Supper as a whole arises from the multifaceted history of interpretation, which the pertinent texts certainly verify for the NT period. The history of interpretation leads to a clear overall view.

Jesus' farewell meal with the Twelve in Jerusalem, on the eve of the Passover in AD 30 or 31, stands at the beginning. In two messianic symbolic acts during this farewell meal Jesus grants the disciples a share in the redemptive power of his impending atoning death and thereby incorporates them into the eschatological table fellowship in God's presence which he anticipates during the meal (Mark 14:25 par.). Then follow the betrayal, the defection of the disciples, Jesus' condemnation and crucifixion, and his burial. After some women who had accompanied Jesus found the tomb opened and empty, and Jesus had appeared as the resurrected one to his disciples in Emmaus and at the Sea of Galilee during a meal, the early Christian meal of thanksgiving of the risen "Lord" (Acts 2:36) is celebrated in Jerusalem in remembrance of Jesus' farewell meal, passion, and resurrection. This "Lord's Supper" correctly becomes detached from the unique Passover date and is celebrated on Sunday, the day of Jesus' resurrection (and perhaps even daily). Already in Jerusalem this meal carries great significance for the church because it unites the believers into the new people of God. From Jerusalem the Lord's Supper celebration moves on to the early Christian mission communities.

Paul receives the authoritative tradition of the Lord's Supper subsequent to his call to apostleship in Damascus, and in Antioch he adopts the (proto-) Lukan tradition of the passion and the Lord's Supper in use there. He delineates the ecclesiastical significance of the Lord's Supper especially in 1 Corinthians 10 and 11. In the celebration of the meal the encounter with the Christ of the gospel, with the reconciler and Lord, receives its greatest symbolic realization possible in this world. At Jesus' table the community is made one with its Lord and with one another in the "body of Christ." The apostle does not conceal from the Corinthians the community's relevant obligation and peril.

The conclusion of the NT interpretation of the Lord's Supper is found in the Gospel of John. Here the meal is already detached from the Passover date and as a sacrament of the resurrection is being defended against Jewish criticism and against scorn from (docetic) Christian pseudofaith. In the food and drink distributed during the meal, Jesus' redemptive mission in the world becomes concrete to the extent that the believers are literally able to taste and experience Jesus' word that opens up eternal life and his being as the Bread of Life. In John the Lord's Supper is placed in relation to the wonderful messianic feeding of the people of God gathered around Jesus. In this way it takes on the significance of being the nourishment of the true Israel, constituted by Jesus, a people on its earthly pilgrimage of witness to the last day, when Jesus will resurrect those sharing the meal with him and will take them to himself to the dwelling places he prepared in his Father's house (John 14:3).

Ever since Jesus' farewell Passover, and beginning with the new inauguration of the celebration of the Lord's meal in Jerusalem, the Lord's Supper of the church has been set in the context of the broad horizons of salvation history. These span from the redemption of the people of Israel from slavery in Egypt, via the remembrance of the redemption of God's new people in the passion and resurrection of Jesus, all the way to the anticipation of the redemption of all believers (Jews and

Gentiles) from affliction, suffering, and death on the last day, through the Parousia of Jesus Christ, the Son of man. Remembrance of the history of salvation and eschatological assurance are mutually dependent in the early Christian meal celebrations. In this manner the gospel of Jesus Christ is made concrete in all of its temporal contexts through the Lord's Supper. The celebration of the Lord's Supper is the festival of the true symbolic realization of the gospel, entrusted to the community of Christ by the crucified and resurrected Christ and to be re-enacted by the community.[34] By means of food and drink those believing in Jesus Christ are united with him as a body at the table of the Lord. When Jesus invites the world to his table and in the meal grants the world a share in his pro-existence, heaven and earth are promising to become one.

As post-Easter testimonial texts all Lord's Supper traditions of the NT are determined by the belief and worship practice of the early Christian communities. Hence they are text components that reflect the Lord's Supper practice of early Christianity. Nevertheless, these texts have different functions.[35] Mark 14 and Luke 22 are narrative texts, which one can imagine were presented in the course of the meal in Jerusalem, Antioch, or Corinth in the framework of the "remembrance" and "proclamation" of Jesus' death. Matthew 26 has already augmented and

---

[34] At this point I can only concur with Oswald Bayer, who argues "that the celebration of the Lord's Supper is the comprehensive presentation of what constitutes the base of the Christian faith, of what it sets its focus on and of what the practice of the community is able to accomplish. Hence it is the event that theology has to consider if the latter intends to be presented comprehensively; in fact theology is shaped and determined by the event. The Lord's Supper is 'a short concept of the entire gospel,' its 'compendium,' its 'sum'—so Martin Luther," "Kurzer Begriff des ganzen Evangeliums: Das Herrenmahl als Mitte des Glaubens," *EK* 12 (1979) 73. On this subject see also idem, "Tod Gottes und Herrenmahl," *ZTK* 70 (1973) 346–63.

[35] In the more recent investigation it has been especially Pesch, "Abendmahl," 34ff., who has drawn attention to the diverse text types and to the functions of the different NT Lord's Supper texts. His text analysis has made it possible, for instance, to move beyond the viewpoint that has become almost canonical in scholarly literature, that Mark 14:22–24 (25) is an interpolation (originating from early Christian liturgy) in the Markan narrative or that all the synoptic institution accounts are to be regarded at once as liturgies in the sense of 1 Cor 11:23ff.

reshaped the Markan account to the extent that it is possible to construe verses 26–29 as having been used liturgically. Finally, one can observe from the Pauline text of 1 Corinthians 11 how a narrative text, originating from the (proto-) Lukan tradition of the passion, has become liturgy and liturgically authoritative tradition by means of which the apostle argues against the Corinthians. In John 6:52–58 John presents an argument-oriented testimonial text toward which Jesus' Bread of Life discourse leads and which defends the Lord's Supper against the critiques of both Jews and Christian Docetists. As long as Christians and Jews lived in close proximity to one another, as long as Jewish and Gentile Christians had common meals, and as long as the Christian community remained aware of its roots in Israel's history, it was possible from the perspective of John 6 and 13 (or even from the Lukan account of Jesus' farewell Passover) to join in the celebration of the Jewish Passover festival in a particular sense: in the penitential fast for Israel on the evening of the Passover and the celebration of the Lord's Supper on the following morning. In the ancient church this practice is attested by the so-called Quartodecimans.

As we have made clear from the beginning, the history of the Lord's Supper celebration that we have sketched and the meaningfulness of the Lord's Supper tradition brought to light thereby are only one part of the liturgical tradition of the church incumbent upon us. A glance at the biblical tradition demonstrates that the form of the Lord's Supper that has become customary in our churches, which is focused on the words of institution and the partaking of bread and wine (as well as the subsequent prayer of thanksgiving from Ps 103), is indeed only a small remainder of a tradition that originally was much fuller and had more extensive correlations. If one sees the Lord's Supper in its biblical fullness, it does indeed emerge as a precious possession and as such could enable the community to attain renewed unity and orientation of life. Because the biblical tradition is also to become authoritative for the contemporary celebrations in the Protestant churches, it is my hope that in our churches too the Lord's Supper celebration might one day be observed again as it was in early Christianity—as a festival of the gospel's true symbolic realization.

Index of Scripture References